WELCOMING GOD'S WORD

Reading With Head and Heart

BILL BAGENTS

CYPRESS

Published by Cypress Publications

Copyright © 2021 by Bill Bagents

Manufactured in the United States of America

Cataloging-in-Publication Data
Bagents, Bill (William Ronald), 1956–
Welcoming God's word: reading with head and heart / by Bill Bagents
p. cm.
Includes scripture index.
ISBN 978-1-087939315 (pbk.) 978-1-087939322 (ebook)
1. Devotional literature. 2. Christian life—Churches of Christ authors. I. Author. II. Title.
BV4801 .B27 2021   242.2—dc20
Library of Congress Control Number: 2021926085
Scripture quotations are from the ESV® Bible (The Holy Bible, English Standard Version®), copyright © 2001 by Crossway, a publishing ministry of Good News Publishers. Used by permission. All rights reserved.
Cover design by Brad McKinnon and Brittany Vander Maas.
All rights reserved. No part of this publication may be reproduced, distributed, stored in a retrieval system, or transmitted in any form or by any means without the prior written permission of the publisher, except in the case of brief quotations embodied in critical reviews and certain other noncommercial uses permitted by copyright law.

Cypress Publications
3625 Helton Drive
PO Box HCU
Florence, AL 35630
www.hcu.edu

Table of Contents

Dedication	viii
Acknowledgements	ix
Bible Abbreviations	x
Introduction	xiii
A New Hearing	1
Ears to Hear	4
Checking Our Hearing	6
Having Eyes to See	8
Rightly Handling the Word of Truth	10
Pulling Out of Scripture What Was Never There	13
Biblical Tensions	16
Respect for the Text: Knowing What We Don't Know	21
Book, Chapter, and Verse	24
Book, Chapter, and Verse for the Restoration Movement	26
Thinking Soberly About Teaching and Preaching	28
How to Listen to a Sermon	30
Claiming to Speak for God	32
Does God Answer All Our Questions?	34
Asking the Right Questions I	36
Asking the Right Questions II	38
Asking the Right Questions III	40
Asking the Right Questions IV	42
Asking the Right Questions V	44

From Questions to Faith	46
The Challenges of Application	48
Struggling with a Passage	51
"And He Shall Direct Your Paths"	56
Comfort and Grace	58
Saved by Grace Through Faith	60
Christians	62
Euodia and Syntyche	64
Evil, Unbiblical, and Counterproductive	67
False Teachers	69
Conflicting Messages	71
"A Fool Gives Full Vent to His Spirit"	73
Providence and Prayer	75
Love Abandoned	78
Things Are Not Always as They Appear	81
Jesus Always Wins	83
The Wrong Kind of Confession	86
Evidences of Inspiration	88
Jacob Wrestling with "God"	91
Sin	93
Does God Still Punish Sin?	95
God Is Better at Forgiving Than We Are at Sinning	98
Obeying the Gospel	100
"And Do not Grieve the Holy Spirit of God"	102
Righteousness and Peace	104

"It Is More Blessed to Give"	107
Change for the Sake of Change, aka Fixing What Isn't Broken	109
If It Ain't Broke	112
Change	115
Childlike or Childish	117
Some Things Require Too Much Faith to Believe	120
The Real Undead	122
Eternally Homeless	124
Where There's Smoke	126
God's Freedom of Speech	128
The Delusions of Power	130
We Don't Know What We Don't Know	132
Will My Life Matter?	134
Did He Really Say That?	136
Honesty Remains the Best Policy	138
No Good Deed	140
Too _____ to Die?	144
"I Was Only Joking"	146
Live Dumb!	148
Things I Can't Wrap My Mind Around	150
Wisdom	152
Choosing an Attitude	155
Reframing	157
Better Than We Deserve	159
Positive Enabling	161

Consistency	163
The Irony of Inconsistency I	165
The Irony of Inconsistency II	167
Consistency and Grace	169
Atmosphere	171
Love	173
Kindness	176
Perspective	178
All the Difference in the World	180
Advantages	182
People Are Something	186
It's Easier to Do Right	189
Life Can Slow You Down	191
Fragile	193
How We Need to Pray!	195
Weather Woes	197
On Storms and Attitudes	199
Sweet Words	201
Saying What We Mean and Meaning What We Say	205
Giving and Keeping Our Word	207
The Destructive Power of Bad Words	209
Lying Liars and Their Lying Lies	212
Words Have Always Been Dangerous	215
A Rare Opportunity	217
Combating Gossip	219

Trouble I	221
Trouble II	223
The Power of Discouragement	225
Discouragement Questions	228
Dead Church	230
On Wounds	233
Self-Inflicted Wounds	236
Dealing with Anger	239
Ironies	242
It's Later Than You Think	245
Closing Another Chapter	247
Closer to Heaven with Each New Year	249
You Can't Be Too Careful?	251
Errors	254
Unfathomable	256
Sadness	259
Suicide: A Stunning Tragedy	261
When People Don't Want Help	264
Pursue Peace	266
Waste Not	268
Good Miss	270
Signs that Faith Is Slipping	272
Protection	274
Lucky Day	276
Doing Good	278

Blessings of Evangelism	280
Scripture Index	282

Dedication

I've been blessed with so many outstanding teachers,
especially Rex Turner, Sr. and W.B. West, Jr.
But to this day, I've learned more Bible from my mother,
Martha Sue Sanders Bagents, than from every one of them.

Acknowledgements

Though all errors are mine to own, Laura Lynn Stegall Bagents read and re-read everything, rescuing me from hoards of mistakes. As both proofreader and wife, she did much more than catching errors. She contributed countless suggestions—regarding both style and content. She won't let me put her name on the book, but everyone knows that we write better together.

This book doesn't exist without the kindness and competence of the staff of Heritage Christian University Press / Cypress Publications. Executive Director Jamie Cox did far more editing than was fair to her. Managing Editor Brad McKinnon has both skills and judgment that I lack. HCU Director of Marketing and Events Brittany Vander Maas assisted notably with the cover.

Bible Abbreviations

Old Testament

Gen	Genesis
Exod	Exodus
Lev	Leviticus
Num	Numbers
Deut	Deuteronomy
Josh	Joshua
Judg	Judges
Ruth	Ruth
1–2 Sam	1–2 Samuel
1–2 Kgs	1–2 Kings
1–2 Chr	1–2 Chronicles
Ezra	Ezra
Neh	Nehemiah
Esth	Esther
Job	Job

Ps	Psalms
Prov	Proverbs
Eccl	Ecclesiastes
Song	Song of Solomon
Isa	Isaiah
Jer	Jeremiah
Lam	Lamentations
Ezek	Ezekiel
Dan	Daniel
Hos	Hosea
Joel	Joel
Amos	Amos
Obad	Obadiah
Jonah	Jonah
Mic	Micah
Nah	Nahum
Hab	Habakkuk
Zeph	Zephaniah
Hag	Haggai
Zech	Zechariah
Mal	Malachi

New Testament

Matt	Matthew
Mark	Mark
Luke	Luke
John	John
Acts	Acts
Rom	Romans
1–2 Cor	1–2 Corinthians
Gal	Galatians
Eph	Ephesians
Phil	Philippians
Col	Colossians
1–2 Thess	1–2 Thessalonians
1–2 Tim	1–2 Timothy
Titus	Titus
Phlm	Philemon
Heb	Hebrews
Jas	James
1–2 Pet	1–2 Peter
1–2–3 John	1–2–3 John
Jude	Jude
Rev	Revelation

Introduction

Oh, how I love your law! It is my meditation all the day. Psalm 119:97

We can't claim to match the passion or poetry of the psalmist, but we know he made a great choice to go "all in" with God's revealed truth. One of the biggest blessings of a life in teaching and preaching is getting to swim in the sea of Scripture each day. The adventure never ends. There's always something new and noteworthy; always something challenging and creative; always something rich, rewarding, and relevant to the needs of the hour.

We know that grasping, applying, and teaching God's word deserves better than our best, but somehow that's not discouraging. Given the rewards of knowing God more fully and being blessed by His wisdom, we keep seeking a better best. It's a noble quest with no top end. The more we learn, the more we want to learn. The more we trust and obey, the more we find ourselves loving and following Jesus. The more we love and follow Jesus, the more passionately we trust and obey. It's remarkable how God makes this work to our benefit.

Because He loves us, God calls us to hear Him well. Because we love Him, we must answer that call. Thus, *Welcoming God's Word—*

a series of invitations to hear God well and to let Him help us live in His grace. Enjoy the adventure.

A New Hearing

We love to invite people to hear the word of God anew, as it were "to hear the truth again for the first time." Hebrews 4:12 supports that effort. The living word remains powerful, piercing, and discerning. It would be horrible to make God's word seem stale or irrelevant.

Hearing anew requires effort. It can't be done while the brain is on autopilot. It necessitates high-level processing. It requires what Jesus called "ears to hear," an openness to spiritual truth and understanding. For two clear examples, see John 2:19–21 and 3:4. As Jesus spoke spiritually, some heard only on an earthly level. And they totally missed God's truth.

Hearing anew demands a certain attitude. It can't be done by a person who already knows it all. Is it possible for the person who thinks he knows it all to really hear anything? Think of John 9, both the assumption of the disciples in verse 2 and the unbelief of the Pharisees as documented in verses 16, 18, and 28–29. The Pharisees were so sure of themselves that new data, even a miracle, could not be considered. The "facts" had to be adjusted to fit their foregone conclusions.

Hearing anew is a Berean concept—remember Acts 17:11. Those fair-minded folks "received the word with all eagerness," but they excelled by also "examining the Scriptures daily to see if these things were so." New doesn't mean errant or divergent. To stay with Acts, we all have the capacity to learn "the way of God more accurately" (Acts 18:26).

Hearing anew isn't just a love for all things new, as if "new" always means improved. Acts 17:21 speaks so clearly to that: "Now all the Athenians and the foreigners who lived there would spend their time in nothing except telling or hearing something new." According to Acts 17:32, even those lovers-of-the-new chose to hear with filters. Some started mocking as soon as Paul preached the resurrection of Christ. Just as all things new aren't true, neither are all things old false. Truth stands the test of time.

Hearing anew has been described in terms of telling the old, old story with fresh words and fresh feeling. Another describes it as translating God's truth for modern minds. Still another suggests that it's inviting the hearer to enter God's world and to be transformed by the encounter. These fit the teachings of Romans 12:1–2 and Colossians 3:16–17. They are at the very heart of Psalm 119.

Yes, caution is warranted in attempting to invite a new hearing of God's truth. Twisted truth isn't truth anymore (2 Pet 3:14–18). If the resurrection is reduced to mere metaphor, it loses its saving power (1 Cor 15:12–19). If the devil is presented as myth, then clear teaching of Jesus is denied (John 8:44, Matt 4). If hell isn't real, then the Bible is not trustworthy.

On the other hand, the story of Jacob, Joseph, and Joseph's brothers reeks of parental favoritism, jealousy, and sibling rivalry. To say so affirms the relevance and timelessness of Scripture. To emphasize the psychological brilliance of Joshua's farewell address, especially the words of Joshua 24:19–20, helps us see both God's guiding hand and some major human tendencies that are true across time and culture. To recognize the worthy wife of Proverbs 31 as an effective manager and a shrewd businesswoman in no way detracts from her faith, her character, or the biblical text.

May God bless us to keep hearing His word anew. May we appreciate thoughtful teachers who try to help us find fresh hearing. Please pray for a heart that wants to hear all that God says.

Ears to Hear

He who has ears, let him hear! Matthew 13:9

Time and again, Jesus emphasized the challenge, importance, and responsibility of accurate hearing. Matthew 13:9 comes at the end of the parable of the sower, which is the first parable in the "parable chapter" of the New Testament. After the last parable of that chapter, Jesus said to them, "Have you understood all these things?" (Matt 13:51). Though they answered, "Yes," it is easy to think that they overestimated themselves. It's a real challenge to hear God accurately. It's a challenge to hear anyone accurately.

Years ago after a visit with my parents, our son John asked what I did on the farm. One of my jobs was to help Uncle Hugh restore a fence that had been destroyed. I told him, "Papa hung a rake in the electric fence, broke several posts, and tore down the barbed wire for an eighth of a mile." John looked highly confused for a moment. Soon he confessed the source of his confusion. He was wondering how an 80-year-old man could pull down a series of posts by hanging a garden rake in the wire. He wasn't thinking of Papa driving a large tractor pulling a hay rake. It wasn't within his frame of reference. He who has ears to hear, let him hear.

It's so easy to assume. A wife says to her husband, "You're spending too much time at the office. Could you please come home on time this week?" What she really means is, "I love to spend time with you. I need to spend time with you. You are the most precious person in my life." But what he "hears" is, "All you do is nag. I work like a dog, and I get criticized for it. Nobody ever appreciates me." What a loss! What a danger!

We love Colossians 4:6, "Let your speech always be gracious, seasoned with salt, so that you may know how you ought to answer each person." It's great and right to practice gracious speech. It's just as right and just as important to practice gracious hearing. One of the ways we know how we "ought to answer each person" is to listen fairly and carefully to each individual. People tell us so much when we have ears to hear. They often tell us how to help them.

We hear contextually and attitudinally. We assume a context based on experience and observation. We evaluate environmental and social cues, often without realizing the work that our brains are doing. We hear best from an attitude of love and respect.

Jesus cares deeply about how we hear (Luke 8:18) and what we hear (Mark 4:24). We need to hear God's truth. We need to hear people's hearts. We need to hear with the aim of helping people toward heaven. We need to hear with love, mercy, and kindness.

We need to check our hearing regularly by listening to God's word. Are we growing more like Jesus? Are we serving and loving others in His name? Are we speaking His truth in love (Eph 4:15)? Are those who hear us being drawn to Christ?

Checking Our Hearing

Take care then how you hear. Luke 8:18

Throughout my preaching life, I have benefited greatly from the kindness of brethren. Countless times people have listened with grace and worked hard to hear a better sermon or class than I was able to present. Many times, brethren have offered helpful suggestions to me.

We value James 3 and recognize that God holds those who teach His word to a higher standard. We are responsible for the words we choose and the attitudes we convey. As we prepare and preach, we're wise to devote much time to prayer and reflection.

We remember the story of a speaker who was greatly disturbed at learning that an aspect of his sermon had been misunderstood by a listener. In this case, it wasn't even what he said. It was that he didn't emphasize a point that the listener had expected. The "omission" seems to have been judged both purposeful and dangerous. Matthew 7:1–5 was tragically forgotten.

Such misunderstandings are not rare. Major reflection is in order. Please weigh the following.

No single verse, class, sermon, or article engages every aspect of a complex and important subject. Time and endurance won't allow such.

We're wise to pay far more attention to what is said rather than what is not said. I know there can be exceptions, but assumptions drawn from the unspoken are so often errant. The positive answers to "Why didn't you cover ____?" range from "I'm saving that for another lesson" to "I'm sorry, but it never crossed my mind."

If a given class, sermon, book, post, or article disappoints us, we're wise to consider the speaker/author's total body of work. Anyone can have a poor day. No one is at his best in every situation. If Matthew 18:15-17, Acts 18:24-28, or Galatians 6:1-2 need to be applied, apply them. Apply them with love and meekness.

Before becoming disappointed in a speaker or author, check your hearing and your reasoning. Did I hear in context? Did I hear in light of Matthew 7:12 and 1 Corinthians 13? Have I added 2 + 2 and reached a false sum? Have I missed a metaphor or some other figure of speech? Has my current situation clouded my hearing or my thinking? Have other wise and mature hearers had the same concerns I have?

We readily admit that a false teacher could use all the items above to mask his purposeful error. If I were a purposeful false teacher, I certainly wouldn't own up to it! I'm not at all suggesting that we hear without judgment and discretion.

We love the Berean approach from Acts 17:11. Value God's word, eagerly receive good teaching, and never forget the biblical version of "trust, but verify." The Bereans kept their orientation positive. They wanted to hear, love, and obey the word of God. They knew that Scripture is trustworthy and authoritative. They took personal responsibility for both how and what they heard. What an example for us! We're blessed to keep our hearing both kind and thoughtful.

Having Eyes to See

Ezekiel 12:2 stands as one of the saddest verses in Scripture: "Son of man, you dwell in the midst of a rebellious house, who have eyes to see but do not see, who have ears to hear, but hear not: for they are a rebellious house." The next verse tells the prophet to prepare his belongings for captivity. The day of God's judgment was at hand.

Recently an exam included having my pupils dilated. As I left the doctor's office, I thought my cheap sunglasses would provide enough help to let me drive to work. They did, but just barely. It would have been smarter to have called for a ride.

Even temporarily impaired vision is a nuisance and a danger. Impaired spiritual vision is far worse. In some cases it is worse because it's voluntary. Ezekiel's peers could have seen the proverbial writing on the wall. They could have read the holy commandments and known that they were in rebellion. But they preferred their path to God's path, so they closed their eyes and plowed on toward destruction.

Impaired spiritual vision is deceitful, progressive, and systemic. Ignoring any part of God's truth makes it easier to close our eyes to the next important teaching and to make the next bad decision. Like David's conduct after his adultery, each step downward seems necessary; it seems to make sense. We know the human tendency to rationalize and cover up.

Impaired spiritual vision can lead to spiritual blindness. We can come to love the darkness (John 3:19–20). We can come to love the darkness so much that God delivers us to it (2 Thess 2:9–12). Those who rebel can come to excuse, accept, or forget their rebellion. Guilt gives way to self-acceptance. Thus, spiritual blindness can sink below the level of our awareness. We don't realize that we have walked away from God into spiritual death.

Ezekiel 12:2 reminds us of a fact that that most of us know through common sense, experience, and observation—our attitude affects our vision. We tend to see what we want to see. We tend to be blind to the inconvenient. Rebels need a path around God's rules, so they close their eyes to His word and find one.

- All of God's rules were written for another time and place; none of them apply to our age.
- God's rules are meant for the less informed; they don't apply to bright people like us.
- God's rules aren't really rules; they're more like suggestions. We need not follow them literally.
- Some of God's rules seem to conflict with others; in such cases we can choose one, the other, or neither (Matt 15:3–9).
- God's rules are too complicated for our understanding; there's no way we can "rightly [handle] the word of truth" (2 Tim 2:15). Why attempt the impossible?

Pretending not to see works just as effectively as pretending to see—pretense isn't reality. Pretense isn't truth. Pretense can be deadly—both physically and spiritually.

Rightly Handling the Word of Truth

Do your best to present yourself to God as one approved, a worker who has no need to be ashamed, rightly handling the word of truth. 2 Timothy 2:15

As the Bible urges us to handle the word of truth correctly, it reminds us that some don't.

2 Peter 3:14–18 candidly tells us that some parts of Scripture are more challenging than others. Sometimes the challenge is one of understanding, but sometimes the challenge lies at a different level. Matthew 4:6 offers an example of the devil himself "quoting" Scripture—purposefully tempting Jesus to misapply His Father's word.

Why would anyone mishandle the word of truth?

Some are not diligent—not properly careful, serious, and thoughtful in their handling of the word (2 Tim 2:15). This can flow from carelessness, laziness, or lack of respect.

Some are untaught (2 Pet 3:16). Perhaps some are willfully ignorant, unwilling to open their minds to the teaching of Scripture. Perhaps others are content to remain at a low level of knowledge and maturity (Heb 5:12–14). Neither condition is either safe or sound.

Some are spiritually unstable (2 Pet 3:16). To use the words of 2 Timothy 3:7, they are "always learning and never able to arrive at a knowledge of the truth." To use the words of Ephesians 4:14, they are "children, tossed to and fro by the waves and carried about with every wind of doctrine, by human cunning, by craftiness in deceitful schemes."

Some mishandle the word by hearing but failing to do—in the words of 2 Timothy 3:5, "having the appearance of godliness, but denying its power." See Matthew 7:21-23 and 23:3 for the Lord's direct strong condemnation of this form of unbelief.

Some mishandle the word by binding burdens on others, while never lifting a finger to help those who struggle (Matt 23:4). This implies a desire to control and manipulate others.

Some confuse the word of God and the traditions of men, either giving equal weight to both or holding human tradition above the word (Matt 15:1-9). This often flows from selfish motives.

Some are just evil and reject the teaching of the word (Jer 36). They refuse to submit to any authority and challenge anything that calls them to submission.

Whatever the motive for mishandling the word of truth, that motive is unwise and unworthy. That motive is dangerous and destructive. To disrespect the word is to disrespect the Spirit who inspired it (2 Pet 1:19-21). To disrespect the word is to disrespect God who gave it (2 Tim 3:14-17). To disrespect the word is to claim that we know more than God and that we don't need His guidance.

2 Timothy 2:15 shows that there is great blessing in "rightly handling the word of truth." Handling the word with respect shows submission to and love for God. Handling the word with respect shows God that we value His approval.

2 Timothy 2:15 offers one more clear implication: there is work involved in "rightly handling the word of truth." We might think first of the work of study, making sure to understand God's message

But we also think of the work of obedience, bringing our thoughts, words, and actions into compliance with God's will. What a challenge! What an opportunity!

Pulling Out of Scripture

What Was Never There

I found a blogpost citing Ephesians 6:13 to be quite strange. It began with these words:

> We have individualized armor that the Holy Spirit designs specifically for us. It fits us perfectly. Your armor will not fit me; my armor will not fit you. David could not put on Saul's armor and beat Goliath. It just did not fit.

I do not cite the source as I wish to offer no insult. I sent the following comment to several friends:

> This is one more strange post to me. There's no hint in the text of individualization of the armor. Can't say that individualization of armor is impossible, but I don't recall that being taught anywhere in the Bible.

It made we wonder if I sometimes have what I consider to be a cool idea and then "imagine" that idea into the text. I sure hope not. God's word and God's people deserve more respect.

The biblical text never says that Saul's armor did not fit David. Rather, the text says, "he had not tested them" (1 Sam 17:39). If that's correct, we make an assumptive leap without realizing it and then confirm our leap with a mis-remembered example. The word deserves a more careful reading.

We want to honor 2 Timothy 2:15 by "rightly handling the word of truth." We want to heed the warning of 2 Peter 3:16 by avoiding any twisting of the Scriptures. We respect the warning of Revelation 22:18–19.

My thinking isn't always accurate, so I thought it good to check with trusted others. My friend Cory Collins offered a perfect reply to my strange comment:

> It's so dangerous to read into and pull out of Scripture what was never there. Then the hearers think, 'Wow! I never saw that before!' Then the speaker or author rises to a higher spiritual plateau because of his incredible insight. Then he needs to come up with something even more creative and inventive, and the beat goes on.

I love and hate that reply. I love its insight, its recognition of and warning against a dangerous process that deceives and addicts. It reminds us of the Athenian philosophers and their friends in Acts 17:21 who seemed to value only the new. New doesn't mean true. Unique and creative don't mean faithful and accurate.

I hate the fact that Cory's fine reply accurately describes an alluring and addictive danger. To "discover" truth in Scripture that God never put there is merely to discover one's own opinion, preference, or imagination. We remember the famous adage, "Just because I think it so doesn't make it so."

We love creativity and view it as a gift from God. We love fresh and engaging presentations of God's truth that help us understand.

At the same time, we reject and repudiate "pulling out of Scripture what was never there." God says all that God says and only what God says. To see more than is present in Scripture or to say more than is taught by Scripture can't be healthy or wise.

Biblical Tensions

One of Ed Gallagher's excellent and memorable chapel lessons at Heritage Christian University examined the tension between Matthew 6:1, "Beware of practicing your righteousness before other people in order to be seen by them" and Matthew 5:16, "...let your light shine before others, so they may see your good works and give glory to your Father who is in heaven." No contradiction or divine confusion was implied; the point was our need to let the Bible say all that it says and to seek authentic application of biblical truth in our daily lives.

Professor Gallagher's lesson invited many questions:

- How do we keep our motives clear and clean as we seek to honor God?
- If a friend compliments us for effective service, have we somehow honored ourselves rather than honoring God?
- If we receive a series of compliments, do we need to tone down our service lest we be tempted to pride?

In addition to inviting questions, the good lesson reminded us of the importance of letting Scripture speak to Scripture. We've often heard the famous statement, "The Bible is its own best interpreter." It also invited consideration of other texts and concepts that need to be considered "in tension," that is in relationship even when that relationship challenges us.

Examples of biblical tensions include the following:

> We are in the world but not of the world (1 John 2:15–17 and 4:4, John 16:33, Col 2:20, 2 Pet 1:4).

> All the Bible is inspired and profitable, but we live under the new covenant (Heb 8:7–13, Col 2:14 with 2 Tim. 3:14–17, Acts 18:24–28, Rom 15:4, 1 Cor 10:11, John 5:39–40).

> We are neither to add to nor take from the word; we must be sure what we do and teach is God-approved (Col 3:17, Rev 22:18–19, Deut 4:2, 12:32). But the synagogue is never commanded nor explicitly described within Scripture, and both Jesus and Paul often worshipped and taught there (Luke 4:16ff).

> Governing authorities are ordained of God (Rom 13), yet government officials killed Jesus and martyred Christians.

> Paul endured the personal tension of wanting to die and be with Christ versus living longer on earth to do Christ's work (Phil 1).

> We find biblical regulation of slavery (Eph 6:5-9, Phlm) while slavery denies both the second greatest commandment (Matt 22:39) and the Golden Rule (Matt 7:12).

> Christians have been moved by God into His son's kingdom

(Col 1:13), yet an ultimate entrance into the kingdom awaits (2 Pet 1:10–11).

The dangers and challenges of riches (Mark 10:23, 1 Tim 6:9–10), yet God made Abraham, Job, David, Solomon, and many others rich.

Submission to one another (1 Pet 5:5) in relation to submission to authority (1 Pet 3:1, 2:13–14).

The circumstantial tension in ancient Corinth of "To the unmarried and the widows I say that it is good for them to remain single"…"but if you do marry [spoken specifically to engaged couples], you have not sinned" (1 Cor 7).

Broader tension of "It is not good that the man should be alone" (Gen 2:18) and "He who finds a wife finds a good thing and obtains favor from the Lord" (Prov 18:22) in relation to Paul's statement in 1 Corinthians 7:8 and 32–33.

The messenger doesn't matter, only the message (Jonah, Phil 1:12–18, Romans 1:17) in relation to Paul's word to Timothy in 1 Timothy 4:11–16.

Guard and protect your influence/reputation (1 Cor 15:33, Prov 22:1 & 22:24, Eccl 7:1) in light of Jesus calling Matthew and eating with Zacchaeus, Jesus eating at a Pharisee's house and Jesus letting a sinful woman wash His feet (Luke 7:36–50).

Servants of God should be an open book, with nothing to hide in relation to Proverbs 29:11, "A fool gives full vent to his spirit, but a wise man quietly holds it back."

Salvation is by grace through faith (Eph 2:8–9) in relation to the clear call to gospel obedience and a life of God-honoring works (Phil 2:12–13, Matt 5:16, 1 Cor 15:58, 1 Pet 1:22 and 4:17).

"Judge not that you be not judged" (Matt 7:1) in relation to "Judge not by appearance, but judge with righteous judgment" (John 7:24). Both are quotes from Jesus.

Proverbs 26:4 in relation to Proverbs 26:5.

The list above is not exhaustive, but it demonstrates that the concept of "biblical tensions" is not rare. What are we to do in light of such tensions? We offer five recommendations.

1. Recognize them, with no hiding and no denying. Choose to deal with reality. Reject the myth that understanding of Scripture will always be easy (2 Pet 3:16).

2. Reflect on them; embrace, explore, and examine. Welcome and wrestle with them. Welcome their ability to make us think. Welcome the humility they engender. Welcome the opportunity to learn, both from God and from fellow learners.

3. Reject false resolution. Do not seek, allow, or imagine

simplistic pseudo-solutions.

4. Refuse to allow the existence of tensions to create discouraging doubt (2 Tim 3:14–17).

5. Respect and revere God as we live in tension. God understands even the inexplicable. No angle or nuance escapes Him.

God lives in perfect peace and tranquility. And if we stay with Jesus, one day we will live in the fullness of His peace as well.

Respect for the Text:

Knowing What We Don't Know

In light of Psalm 119, 2 Timothy 3:14-17, 2 Peter 1:19-21, and Revelation 21:18-19, we hold the Bible in high esteem. What the Bible teaches, we believe. That said, we also acknowledge that Scripture can be misused and misunderstood. The Bible makes this clear.

The call to diligence in 2 Timothy 2:15 speaks of "rightly handling the word of truth." If truth can be "rightly handled," there's strong implication that it can be dealt with wrongly—whether misunderstood or misapplied.

We remember Peter's comment on Paul's inspired writings "There are some things in them that are hard to understand which the ignorant and unstable twist to their own destruction, as they do the other scriptures" (1 Pet 3:16).

Satan used Scripture in His effort to tempt Jesus (Matt 4:6). And the very words of Jesus were misunderstood by some disciples who heard Him directly (John 21:20).

Even we who highly respect Scripture face temptations in realizing the limits of our knowledge and understanding. The book of Esther offers two outstanding examples of our tendency to think that we know more than the text says.

In Esther 1, Queen Vashti refuses a royal order to appear before the King's officials "with her royal crown, in order to show the peoples and the princes her beauty ..." (Esth 1:10). Alcohol was involved in the request. We don't know why or with what attitude she refused. Speculation abounds:

- She thought it improper to appear before a drunken group.
- She thought appearing to show off her beauty was demeaning.
- She didn't like to be commanded.
- She and the king were having problems, and she wanted to show him up.

We don't know because the text does not say. We need to know that we don't know.

In Esther 3, Mordecai refused to bow before Haman as King Ahasuerus commanded. He refused even when asked, "Why do you transgress the king's command?" (Esth 3:3) Again, the text gives no reason for Mordecai's refusal. Speculation includes:

- He knew Haman's character—his pettiness and arrogance. He didn't want to feed the pride.
- The Lord had told Mordecai to refuse to bow, thereby setting up the conflict that would show God's ability to protect and deliver His people through providential means.
- Mordecai was just as human as the rest of us. He didn't bow because he didn't want to.

Again, we don't know because the text does not say. There is no harm in discussing possible reasons, but conclusive answers won't be found because God didn't choose to provide them.

The older I get, the more content I am to say in such matters, "I don't know because the Bible doesn't say." If the Lord had wanted us to know, He'd have told us. If it mattered to our well-being or our salvation, He would have told us. I also don't know what the mark on Cain's head looked like, I don't know what manna tasted like, I don't know what Jesus looked like, and I don't know what Jesus wrote on the ground (John 8:1–11). And not knowing doesn't trouble me one bit.

Book, Chapter, and Verse

Whenever we're asked to give book, chapter, and verse for a teaching or practice, our first thought is one of appreciation. For many good people, requesting book, chapter, and verse is shorthand for asking, "Can you demonstrate scriptural authority for what you are teaching and doing?" We cannot overstate the nobility of that essential question.

Jesus Himself recognized the legitimacy of godly authority. Matthew 21:23 records the critics' question, "By what authority are you doing these things, and who gave you this authority?" Jesus did not reject their question. Knowing that a trap was being laid, He answered with a question, a question of authority.

> I also will also ask you one question, and if you tell me the answer, then I also will tell you by what authority I do these things. The baptism of John, from where did it come? From heaven or from man? (Matt 21:24–25)

In every way, Jesus recognized and upheld the authority of the Father (Matt 26:36–42, John 8:29 and 9:4, Phil 2:8, Heb 5:8). We walk in the steps of Jesus when we uphold the truth of Colossians 3:17. We heed the warning of Jesus when we reject the lawlessness of adding to or subtracting from God's word (Matt 7:21–27, Deut 4:2, Prov 30:6).

As much as we value and support the concept of having biblical authority for all that we teach and practice in the name of Christ, there is a way that the request for book chapter, and verse is sometimes misused. Some seem to have the errant notion that every doctrine and practice must flow from a single verse or text. They reject the concept that some truth flows from the whole of biblical teaching. They forget that the whole of Scripture must be allowed to speak on every biblical subject. They forget that while Scripture strongly demands establishing scriptural authority for doctrine and practice, no passage of Scripture directly demands "book, chapter and verse." Scripture could not do so. Chapter and verse numbers were added as study and memory aids centuries after the text was written.

For example, the whole biblical doctrine of salvation cannot be found in a single verse or text, not even the beloved John 3:16 or Romans 5:6–11. Neither passage directly speaks of confession—identified as essential in Matthew 10:32–33, repentance—identified as essential in Acts 17:30, or of putting on Christ in baptism—identified as essential in Romans 6:4–6. The biblical doctrines of the Trinity, of worship, and of church leadership are not one-verse or one-passage doctrines. To demand biblical authority for religious doctrine and practice is noble and right. To demand single verse or single passage authority for a doctrine or practice is neither. What the whole Bible says on any subject is relevant. What every applicable passage says is important. To act without biblical authority is rebellion. To demand a standard for biblical authority which the Bible does not set is also rebellion. To walk humbly with our God is life, peace, and faithfulness (Mic 6:8).

Book, Chapter, and Verse for the Restoration Movement

We once received a most interesting request: "Please give book, chapter and verse for the Restoration Movement, and please explain how a church that can't be destroyed can be restored." The response that we offered is below. Perhaps you can make it even stronger.

There is no single book, chapter, and verse—by name—demanding a "Restoration Movement." However, the concept of restoration is clearly taught in Scripture. Jeremiah 6:16 calls the faithful to "ask for the ancient paths, where the good way is" so that they can be approved by God. Jeremiah 18:15 decries those who have stumbled in their ways, forsaking "the ancient roads … to walk into side roads, not the highway." The idea is that they have left God's path. Those who have ceased walking correctly need to restore their former walk.

2 Kings 22–23 documents Josiah's restoration. The Book of the Law was found during remodeling (restoration) of the temple. Upon reading, the leaders of God's people learned that they were noncompliant with God's revealed will. They needed, and Josiah led them in, restoration. They admitted their error. They recognized the truth of God's word. They repented and changed their behavior. 2 Chronicles 7:14 similarly describes the human role in biblical

restoration.

Please consider Revelation 2:4–5, 2:14–16, 3:2–3, and 3:14–22. Congregations had left their first love, tolerated error, and grossly overestimated their standing before God. They needed the positive change of repentance. They needed restoration to God's ideal, to God's standard.

In terms of explaining how a church that can't be destroyed can be restored, Revelation 3:1 says the church at Sardis was dead. However, the next verses reveal that this was not an absolute statement. They were called to "strengthen what remains." Though the church, overall, was "dead," Revelation 3:4 reminds us that some were still alive. We think of a fire, largely extinguished, but a coal or a few embers remain.

Restoration does not imply a belief that the church built by Jesus was dead prior to some "restoration movement" (Matt 16:13–19). We cannot rightly claim to know that the Lord's church completely ceased to exist at any point in history. God has not given us that knowledge.

As the term "restoration movement" is used to describe faithful application of the passages listed above and manifests itself in attempts to leave human additions to the doctrine and work of the church by returning to the purity and simplicity of the New Testament pattern for the church, we appreciate the term. It conveys a noble and biblical concept. Seeking to understand, believe, practice, and teach what God commands and exemplifies in Scripture shows respect for God. Showing respect for God is always right.

Thinking Soberly
About Teaching and Preaching

For by the grace given to me, I say to everyone among you, not to think of himself more highly than he ought to think, but to think with sober judgment, each according to the measure of faith that God has assigned. Romans 12:3

Sometimes preachers and teachers are blessed to present a homerun sermon or class. Everything clicks. The illustrations energize. Memory functions perfectly. The hearers connect and visibly engage, the lesson flows, and it feels great.

When that happens, we're blessed to enjoy the moment. And we're blessed to remember that this moment was a blessing from God. If the sermon was faithful, it flowed from His life-changing word (Rom 10:14–17, 2 Tim 3:14–17). If the class was powerful, the power flowed from the gospel (Rom 1:16–17). If the lesson was beneficial, God was the true source of the blessing (James 1:17). And we were blessed by God to be an instrument of His grace.

If we're not careful, the devil will rob us of such moments. He will tempt us to pride. He will ask us to think, "I did well. I thought well. I created something special. I made this work." He will help us avoid thinking of Luke 12:16–21 and Romans 12:3. He will insist that we forget Acts 12:20–24. He will invite us to put ourselves ahead of God.

If that doesn't work, the devil will try the opposite. He will tempt us to fear or to false humility. He will ask us to think, "I can't enjoy this moment. If I enjoy it, then I'm claiming to be something special. If I enjoy it, I'm thinking too highly of myself." He will help us avoid thinking of Acts 18:27–28 and 1 Thessalonians 1:13. He will insist that we forget 2 Thessalonians 2:13–14. He will invite us to declare ourselves unfit to serve the Lord.

I love homerun lessons whenever they come. But I want to remember the following:

What I think to be a homerun may not be. While we want to do our best for God, God often does much with little. I should be grateful for the opportunity to try.

No one does homerun lessons every time. There's virtually no limit to human frailty. We need to pray for God's wisdom, strength, and guidance.

What's a homerun sermon to some hearers may be of far less benefit to others. It's not that the word is weak, but our hearing—like our teaching—is far from perfect. No lesson connects equally well for every hearer.

We're blessed to learn from failures and successes. If a lesson didn't work, why not? How could it be improved? Was it a failure of prayer? Of study? Of attitude? If it worked, how can that lead us to even more effective service to the Lord?

How to Listen to a Sermon

Pay attention to what you hear ... Mark 4:24

Take care then how you hear ... Luke 8:18

Active listening is an art, a skill, a habit, and a blessing. It challenges and encourages both listener and speaker. Like most good things, it doesn't just happen. It's wise to ask ourselves, "How can I improve my listening, especially when God's word is being taught?" The following suggestions offer a start.

Prepare to listen well by having a willing heart (Acts 17:11). If you know the text in advance, read over it—thoughtfully—several times (Ps 1:2). Prepare to listen well by praying for the speaker and for your ability to understand and apply (Matt 13:19).

If physically gathered with the saints, prepare to listen well by arriving early and sitting up front. It's not required, but it diminishes distractions and encourages the preacher. Harried, hurried people seldom listen well.

Prepare to listen well by singing enthusiastically. Singing is part of God's teaching and our teaching one another (Col 3:16-17). Worship wasn't built for casual or partial participation.

Many find that taking notes helps them listen and remember. It enhances our opportunity for further study. Read the passages cited by the preacher from your own Bible. It's the Berean thing to do

(Acts 17:11).

Think as you listen. The Bible is remarkably pro-thinking (Ps 1). What is the key idea of the passage that has just been read? What encouragement is there for us? What opportunity? What blessing? What warning? What call to action? What other passages should be read along with today's text?

Remember the importance of the opportunity! Any teaching of God's word deserves respectful hearing (Neh 8:1–12, John 8:31–32, Rom 1:16).

Ask yourself, "With whom can I share the message from God that I heard today?" Follow the examples of Andrew and Philip (John 1:35–51). Give people the blessing of hearing Jesus.

Claiming to Speak for God

The people of Jeremiah's day suffered from double trouble. On one hand, they failed to listen to the prophets that God sent to them (Jer 44:4–5). They didn't listen because they were not being told what they wanted to hear. On the other hand, they chose to believe the errant messages of false prophets (Jer 27:9–11). They believed the message that they preferred. Yet God's instruction to them was clear. "Do not listen to the words of the prophets, for it is a lie that they are prophesying to you … I have not sent them" (Jer 27:14–15). Sadly, that message is still needed today.

False prophets abound. Year after year, virtually every disaster, whether man-made or natural, energizes them. Think of the Twin Towers on 9.11, the terrible earthquake that devastated Haiti, the most recent tsunami, the horrific explosion in Beirut, or even COVID-19. Some well-known television preacher thinks that he knows the specific causation. The disaster is God's specific, physical judgment on the victims. Their sufferings flow directly from their sins. And we have been spared because we are righteous. On top of that, since their suffering flows from God's judgment of their sin, we have no obligation to help them. And if a disease is involved, the false teachers may even offer to sell us a cure.

Of such messengers we say, "Do not listen to them. God has not sent them. They have invented their message."

Even when the latest victims are political or economic enemies of our nation, as Christians we are free to love them, to pray for them, and to feed them when they're hungry (Matt 5:43–48, Rom 12:14). We are free to "do good to all ..." (Gal 6:10). Like the Good Samaritan, we are not obligated to determine whether or not people in need deserve our help (Luke 10). We are free to help them just because they need us.

As I think of these television and internet preachers, I think of Luke 13:1–5. Some in Jesus' day thought they knew why Pilate killed some of their countrymen as they worshiped. Jesus' response indicates that He heard their underlying message: "They must have deserved it." Jesus' response is as courageous as it is accurate. We all deserve it. Unless we repent, we "will all likewise perish."

Jesus deftly moved the discussion from the physical to the spiritual. He invited those who "were present at that very time" to look inward and upward, to think about their souls. He invites us to do the same.

I deny that modern evangelists have direct revelation from God. They make too many errors. I deny that God has told them why the earthquake or explosion or pandemic happened. And what of the next earthquake, fire, flood, cancer, or shooting near us? Is that, too, a sign of God's judgment? What if it's their building that burns or their plane that crashes?

It's so easy to claim to speak for God. It's so easy to offer opinion as if it were truth. It's so easy to say more than God's word says. But it's always tragically wrong to do so.

Does God Answer All Our Questions?

I heard a well-intentioned speaker say, "God always answers our questions; we've just got to ask the right questions." The first part of that statement kicked my limited critical thinking skills into high gear. I know the second part is just as important and will be contemplated later. But the question of the moment is "Does God always answer our questions?"

Biblically speaking, has God always answered all the questions put to Him? No. Job stands as an outstanding example. Job 30 is labeled in some Bibles as "God does not answer me." It's an accurate chapter heading, flowing directly from Job 30:20, "I cry to you for help, and you do not answer me. ..." The chapter heading for Job 38 commonly reads, "The Lord answers Job." In a sense, it, too, is accurate. It flows from Job 38:1, "Then the Lord answered Job out of the whirlwind. ..." The Lord answered Job in the sense that He responded. But the Lord's response was a magnificent series of questions. To the best of our knowledge, the Lord never told Job the reasons for his sufferings. He never told Job about Satan's challenge.

Biblically speaking, did Jesus answer all the questions put to Him? Isaiah 53:7 prophesied that He would not:

> He was oppressed, and he was afflicted. Yet, he opened not His mouth, like a lamb that is led to the slaughter, and like a sheep before its shearers is dumb, so he opened not is

mouth.

Before Caiaphas and Pilate, He gave no answer to the charges raised against Him (Matt 26:62-63 and 27:13-14). Jesus flatly refused to answer a question put to Him by the chief priests and elders as recorded in Matthew 21:23-27. On many occasions, Jesus answered a question with a question or answered a better question than the one posed to Him.

Is it possible for God to answer all our questions? Even when on earth in the flesh, Jesus couldn't tell His disciples everything that they needed to know. It's not that Jesus was unable. Rather, John 16:12 records the Lord's words: "I still have many things to say to you, but you cannot bear them now." We wonder how true that is for each of us. What could God tell us through His word and providence if we had more capacity to hear and understand? Do we sometimes misinterpret God's silence or "delay"? Do we sometimes overestimate our ability to grasp God's answers? Wouldn't we be wise to thank God for knowing better than we know, even if that leaves some questions unanswered?

We're certain that God does not owe us an answer to any question. He is the Lord, the Creator. He owes us nothing, not even explanation. Could it be that He leaves some questions unanswered just to remind us of that fact? God is always God. God is always good. God is always right. We're always wise to trust Him, even if He doesn't answer every question that we pose.

Asking the Right Questions I

We have previously established two key ideas: (1) contrary to popular belief, God does not answer every question that we ask, and (2) bad questions exist. As surely as bad questions exist and should be avoided, asking the right questions can bless us in countless ways. Correspondingly, failing to ask the right questions at the right time leaves us open to great harm.

Joshua 9 tells the story of the Gibeonites. They heard what happened to Jericho and Ai. They had no illusion that they could overcome God's people in battle. So they decided to change the playing field. They dressed in old clothes, carried old sacks and old wineskins. They approached the Israelites pretending to be ambassadors from a distant land. Under false pretenses, they negotiated a treaty that spared their lives. The Bible clearly states the reason that the deception worked: "so the men took some of their provisions, but did not ask counsel from the Lord" (Josh 9:14). Failing to ask God was a serious mistake.

Joshua was an outstanding leader. He showed great wisdom in so many challenging situations. Why did he fail to seek God's counsel in the case of the Gibeonites? It has been suggested that Joshua and his peers put too much trust in their eyes. They thought they could see that their poor visitors were who they claimed to be—that they were no threat. What a classic illustration of 1 Samuel 16:7, "… For the Lord does not see as man sees; for man looks at the outward appearance, but the Lord looks at the heart."

Others have suggested that Joshua and his peers put too much trust in their power of reasoning. The messengers from Gibeon appeared to be poor travelers from a distant land. There were no contradictory data. They approached the leaders of Israel with humility, saying, "We are your servants" (Josh 9:8). They came with praise for God and knowledge of His work (Josh 9:9–10). Everything they said sounded so right! It's so easy to believe others, especially when they seem to tell us exactly what we already believe.

Some have suggested that the story of the Gibeonites reminds us of the need for cynicism, that we should always doubt the motives and veracity of others. That's not true, but this story teaches us some important truths about our need to ask questions. In many ways, "… the sons of this world are more shrewd in dealing with their own generation than the sons of light" (Luke 16:8). James 1:5 always applies to each of us: "If any of you lack wisdom, let him ask of God, who gives generously to all without reproach, and it will be given him." Compared to the sons of this world, we often lack wisdom. Being baptized does not infuse us with wisdom. Compared to God, we all always lack wisdom. We always need to ask. And being in Christ, we're in the perfect position to ask in humility and faith (Jas 1:6).

Asking the Right Questions II

We constantly need to ask for God's wisdom and guidance. James 1:5 and Proverbs 3:5-6 clearly establish this truth. Proverbs 3:5 offers such clear contrast: Either we can trust in the Lord with all our heart or we can lean on our own understanding. Whom do we deem smarter, self or God? Whom do we deem wiser, self or God? Whom do we deem more consistent, self or God? If we ask those questions, we'll point ourselves in the right direction!

There's great temptation to be wise in our own eyes (Prov 3:7). We tend to overestimate our wisdom, our goodness, and our knowledge. Those who overestimate themselves have no need to inquire of God; they believe that they already know all that really matters. On our better days, we know better. We need to know better every day.

Scripture is filled with examples of people who asked the right question at the right time. Each questioner demonstrated humility and wisdom. Each was blessed by asking God for help. Please consider the example below.

We assume that the servant, identified as "the oldest servant" of Abraham's house, was Eliezer of Damascus (Gen 15:2 and 24:2). He was given such a daunting task. He was to find a wife for Isaac, Abraham's son of promise. As he reached Abraham's homeland and began his work, this servant said to God, "O Lord, God of my master Abraham, please grant me success today, and show steadfast love to my master Abraham" (Gen 24:12). He asked the Lord. He asked unselfishly. He asked boldly and specifically. And God answered—"before he had finished speaking" (Gen 24:15)! While we cannot claim that every answer will come so quickly or clearly, this one did.

To his credit, Abraham's servant remembered that God was blessing him. Upon realizing that he had met Abraham's relatives, "The man bowed his head and worshiped the Lord and said, 'Blessed be the Lord the God of my master Abraham ...'" (Gen 24:26-27, 52). The servant asked, the Lord blessed, the servant worshiped and gave thanks, and God continued to bless. What an encouraging cycle!

Many overemphasize the patriarchal nature of the Bible, particularly the Old Testament. Leadership in home and government was overwhelmingly provided by men, but the idea that ladies had no rights and were treated as chattel is severe overstatement. Genesis 24:52ff makes this clear. Rebekah is not commanded to accompany the servant. Rather, she is asked, "Will you go with this man?" What a wise approach! The question communicates respect. It allows Rebekah to choose her future. It lets her make a genuine decision. It prevents the potential pain of second-guessing what was done to her. It allows her to step up to the opportunity that God put before her. There's power in questions!

Asking the Right Questions III

There's power in questions! After the fall, Adam and Eve "hid themselves from the presence of the Lord God…" (Gen 3:8). At least, that was their intent. The irony is stunning! How do you hide yourself from the omnipresent, all-seeing Lord?

As God reached out to Adam and Eve, He began with a question, "Where are you?" (Gen 3:9) God knew where they were. Adam's response indicates that he knew that God knew his location. Adam didn't tell God where he was. Rather, he told God why he was hiding.

God continued with two questions. "Who told you that you were naked? Have you eaten from the tree of which I commanded you not to eat?" (Gen 3:11) Adam recognized the rhetorical nature of these questions. He didn't answer either of them. Rather, he offered God an excuse for his disobedience. Eve tried the same approach as recorded in Genesis 3:13.

It's amazing what God accomplished through these questions. He opened a door and created a context for communication. He gave Adam and Eve opportunity to explore their actions and the implications of those deeds. He gave them opportunity to express their thoughts, motives, and needs.

Regrettably, neither Adam nor Eve seized the opportunity that God offered. Each retreated into a defensive posture. Neither said to God, "I have sinned. I have broken Your law. I have disrespected

You." Neither asked for pardon, grace, or help.

The Lord asked the right questions. Nothing that He does falls short of perfection. But, even the best of questions can be thwarted. What kept Adam and Eve from being more open with God? What kept them from answering more fully and faithfully?

Isaiah 59 did not become true when the Spirit inspired Isaiah to write it. The principle taught there has always been true.

> Behold, the Lord's hand is not shortened, that it cannot save, nor his ear dull, that it cannot hear; but your iniquities have made a separation between you and your God, and your sins have hidden his face from you (Isa 59:1).

Sin separates. Iniquity renders people unable to see God as Savior and Friend. Even though God asked the right questions to the right people at the right time, sin kept them from hearing those questions as opportunities to repent.

Were Adam and Eve blinded by pride, by fear, or by guilt? Could all three have been in play? Whatever the case, they tried to avoid facing the truth. They failed. No one can avoid the piercing, pertinent questions of God the righteous judge. And there's no reason to try. Even as judge, God is our only hope. We must come clean with Him!

Asking the Right Questions IV

Abram was in obvious pain. The Lord had called him from his homeland to an unnamed land of promise (Gen 12:1–3). The Lord had promised to make him a great nation and a blessing to every family on earth. Since Abram took God at His word, there should be nothing but smooth sailing ahead. At least that's the way that some now tell the story. We need to be careful of such teachers! Following God is not the end of all trouble.

Reality wasn't nearly so smooth. Even as Abram faithfully journeyed, a famine sent him to Egypt (Gen 12:10–13). Egypt posed new dangers (Gen 12:14–20). Even Abram's financial prosperity came at the cost of strife between his servants and Lot's (Gen 13). Though God repeated the promise of descendants, still no child blessed Abram and Sarai's home (Gen 13:14–16). Lot made bad choices that led Abram into war (Gen 14). Trouble and aggravation followed disappointment and delay.

As we join Abram in Genesis 15, we find him in obvious pain. When God said to him, Do not be afraid, Abram. I am your shield, your exceedingly great reward," Abram must have been surprised. He responded to God, "O Lord God, what will You give me, for I continue childless, and the heir of my house is Eliezer of Damascus?" (Gen 15:2).

We have no trouble following Abram's logic. Lord, you promised me descendants sufficient to be called a great nation, but I don't have a single child. Lord, you gave me great riches, but what good are they without a son or a homeland?

Some are shocked to see Abram, the father of the faithful, in such pain and doubt. It's so easy to forget that Abram was just as human as we are. He had to learn to trust God just like we do. His journey was a journey of faith, just like ours is.

When we read Genesis 15, we love Abram's courage. He didn't suffer in silence. He didn't pretend to feel better than he felt. Just like David in the Psalms, Abram put his pain into words. He asked God the question that most needed to be asked.

We appreciate Abram's courage, and we appreciate his wisdom. Abram directed his question to the one capable of answering. He posed his question to the one who made the promise and raised his hopes. He minced no words and hid no motives when he asked, "O Lord God, what will you give me …?" (Gen 15:2) He asked bluntly and respectfully, addressing God as "Lord." Abram asked, but he didn't demand, demean, or scold.

After Abram asked, he listened. Consider Genesis 15:4–5. God powerfully reaffirmed His promise. And Abram powerfully chose to believe the Lord! Genesis 15:6 is one of the richest and most victorious verses in all of Scripture. Abram asked the right question to the right person. And he listened to and believed God's answer! How amazingly wise!

Asking the Right Questions V

The whole episode with Abram, Sarai, and Hagar disappoints us. On one level, we understand. God promised children, but none came. Sarai wanted a child so badly that she decided to "help God." Like all attempts to run ahead of God, unintended consequences made a mess of things (Gen 16:4–5). Bad attitudes led to harshness, and harshness led Hagar, even though she was pregnant, to run away.

As Hagar fled from Sarai, the angel of the Lord found her and posed two perfect questions. "Hagar, servant of Sarai, where have you come from, and where are you going?" (Gen 16:8) In this encounter, the angel of the Lord teaches us so much about effective communication and about faith.

The angel addressed Hagar by name and by place. He knew who she was as an individual and who she was in relation to God's plan and God's chosen family. He wanted Hagar to remember that truth as well. She had a role to play. Even though her role included submission and suffering, the angel promised God's blessings if Hagar would obey His will. The angel gave meaning and hope to Hagar's situation. It's amazing what people can endure and overcome when they find meaning and hope.

The first question is the easy one: "Where have you come from?" Hagar didn't hear that as a geographical question. She heard it as a question of motive or intention. She was fleeing her angry mistress.

It's as if Hagar had said to herself, "Anywhere is better than here. It just can't get any worse." If she thought that, she was decisively wrong. As we remember Genesis 21:15–21, we find Hagar learning that lesson. When we move before God wants us to move, terrible things can happen.

The second question carries more challenge. "Where are you going?" (Gen 16:8) Hagar could have answered that question with a single word, "Away." The text offers no hint as to her destination. It's as if she didn't have a clue. She just ran.

Pain can do that to people. It can rob us of good judgment. It can make us thoughtless and rash. It can make us dangerously shortsighted. It can cause us to move when there's nowhere to go. It can cause us to act without first seeking God's counsel and will.

Hagar returned to serve Sarai. She returned because she believed the promises that the angel made. She returned because she put the good of her unborn child before her own welfare. She returned because she wanted a better life for her son. And more than 4,000 years later we find that noble and encouraging. The right questions helped Hagar. Asking, contemplating, and answering the right questions can still help us today.

From Questions to Faith

Genesis 16 ends with Hagar's beautiful statement of faith: "So she called the name of the Lord who spoke to her, 'You are a God of seeing,' for she said, 'Truly here have I also seen him who looks after me'" (Gen 16:13).

Hagar didn't really know that the Angel of the Lord was the Angel of the Lord. Not to be silly, but he didn't wear a name tag. He didn't introduce himself to Hagar. He just showed up and started talking. The Angel was on a mission and wasted no time.

Even though Hagar didn't know that the Angel of the Lord was the Angel of the Lord, she knew that he was no mere man. She'd never seen him before, but he knew her name and her occupation. He knew that she was pregnant. He knew that the child would be a son. He knew the name that should be given to the baby. And he knew the baby's destiny. On God's behalf, he even promised great blessings to the boy.

The Angel of the Lord reminded Hagar of the all-seeing eye of God. The Lord not only heard her affliction (Gen 16:11), He also saw it. As Abram named their son Ishmael—heard by God—Hagar gained a lasting reminder of God's knowledge and His concern.

Hagar's response to being seen by God fascinates us. She didn't feel violated. She didn't seek to hide. She didn't fall into denial by pretending that God didn't see. Rather, she chose to name the God who was blessing her. The name she chose is accurate: "You are a

God of seeing." He sees all, but He also sees each individual. He sees us in our triumphs and in our darkest hours. And He acts on what He sees.

Hagar didn't see the whole picture; she didn't know all that God reveals to us in the inspired text. But we respect Hagar for respecting God as represented by His Angel. We respect her for rightly recognizing the spiritual significance of what had just happened to her. While we're respecting Hagar, we also appreciate the fact that the Holy Spirit chose to present this Egyptian lady in such a favorable light. She wasn't any less human, spiritual, or important because she was a servant, female, and Egyptian. She mattered to God.

Hagar didn't see the whole picture; none of us does. But she saw something of God as she interacted with His Angel. The Angel's faithful actions and unique knowledge led Hagar to think of God, to appreciate God, and perhaps even to recognize something of the omnipresence and omniscience of God.

Hagar's question may also remind us of that desire to see God that lives in each of our hearts. God has—and will surely fulfill—the desire that each of use has to see Him (John 14:9, Rom 1:20, 1 John 3:1–3). It's a desire that thrills, motivates, challenges, and encourages each of us.

The Challenges of Application

As believers who love the Lord, we are dedicated to loving, learning, and living His word. Scripture repeatedly makes this abundantly clear.

Deuteronomy 6 urged ancient Israel to observe, keep, teach, and emphasize God's word. Doing so invited God's blessings, showed respect for God, and demonstrated love for Him.

Deuteronomy 10:12–13 similarly links love for God with choosing "to walk in all His ways" and "to keep the commandments and statutes of the Lord."

In Matthew 7:21–23, Jesus defines failing to do God's will as lawlessness which leads to God's rejection. In Matthew 7:24–27, Jesus describes both the solid foundation of hearing "these words of Mine and doing them" and the hopelessness of hearing "these words of Mine" and failing to do them. John 12:48 speaks with stunning clarity: "The one who rejects me and does not receive my words has a judge; the word that I have spoken will judge him on the last day."

As believers who love the Lord and are dedicated to loving, learning, and living His word, we appreciate the challenge and gravity of 2 Timothy 2:15: "Do your best to present yourself to God as one approved, a worker who has no need to be ashamed, rightly handling the word of truth." This passage offers several clear implications.

We face the danger of being less than diligent—less than careful, less than thoughtful and serious with God's word. The word of God is not a toy to be played with.

In that God's word of truth can be "rightly handled," it can be handled wrongly. As surely as we seek God's approval, God's disapproval and personal shame await those who do not deal rightly with His word. God will uphold and defend His word. Biblical examples include Matthew 4:5–6 and 2 Peter 3:14–16. Jesus saw through Satan's effort to use God's word against Him. Peter clearly warns of the connection between mishandling Scripture and personal destruction.

We know God's word can be loved, learned, and lived. We also know that we sometimes face great challenges in discerning and applying its teachings. Some in Jesus' day could easily have reasoned, "Though God originated government for human protection, it would be wrong to pay taxes to the corrupt and pagan Roman system." Yet we know the words of Jesus from Matthew 22:21. His words make it clear that one could pay his taxes without supporting sin and inviting God's judgment. In His infinite wisdom, God never puts us in an impossible bind (1 Cor 10:13).

We respect the need for biblical authority as taught in Matthew 5:17–20, 21:23–27, and 1 Peter 4:11. Some in Jesus' day accused His disciples of breaking "the tradition of the elders" (Matt 15:1–2) without realizing that human tradition can't hold a candle to the commandment of God. Matthew 23 scathingly denounces religious games played by human rulers. We honor God's authority with mercy and humility in our hearts.

Romans 13:1–7 challenges many believers amid political turmoil and confusion. God has always been bigger than politics or government. We submit to every law unless it orders disobedience to God (Acts 4:19 and 5:29). We show respect even when we disagree with those who lead (1 Pet 2:17). We seek to rightly understand, apply, and teach God's word because we love and respect God.

Struggling with a Passage

...If my people who are called by my name humble themselves, and pray and seek my face, and turn from their wicked ways, then I will hear from heaven and will forgive their sin and heal their land. 2 Chronicles 7:14

We know the Old Testament has major value for believers of all time. "For whatever was written in former days was written for our instruction. That through endurance and through the encouragement of the Scriptures we might have hope" (Rom 15:4). The "sacred writings" that Timothy knew from his childhood were able to make him "wise for salvation through faith in Christ Jesus" (2 Tim 3:14–17). Certainly, these writings were what we know as the Old Testament. The Scriptures that Apollos used as "he powerfully refuted the Jews in public, showing by the Scriptures that the Christ was Jesus" were also the Old Testament (Acts 18:28).

We know that 2 Chronicles 7:14 was originally spoken to Solomon about Israel, God's single, unique, chosen nation among all the nations of the ancient world. Though Solomon was their earthly king, God was the King of His theocracy.

We don't for a moment doubt the principles taught in the verse. Proverbs 14:34, Galatians 6:7–9, and countless examples from Scripture and history support the truth that God blesses those who turn to Him. The book of Jonah supports the truth that God delights in blessing the penitent. Correspondingly, we know that "the way of the treacherous is their ruin" (Prov 13:15) because God opposes those who oppose Him (Prov 3:34, Jas 4:6–8, 1 Pet 5:5–11). This is true for nations, churches, families, and individuals (Rev 2:16).

So where's the struggle with 2 Chronicles 7:14? In part, it's a realization that no political state, even a nation as blessed as the USA, is God's chosen people in the Christian age (Romans 9–11; Acts 10–11, particularly 10:34ff). The kingdom of Christ "is not of this world" (John 18:36). We believe with all our heart that God moves those who put on Christ in baptism "to the kingdom of his beloved Son" (Col 1:13–14, Acts 2:47, Eph 2:1–10, Gal 3:26–29). As much as we love our nation, we are not—as ancient Israel was—the single, unique people called by God's name.

Part of our struggle with this ever more popular verse can be expressed as a series of questions.

When we read 2 Chronicles 7:14 from the perspective of a citizen of any modern political state, what are we asserting about other nations? Are we saying that our nation is more "chosen" than other nations?

When we read 2 Chronicles 7:14 from the perspective of any modern nation, what are we saying about fellow Christians who are citizens of other nations? Do they hear us to be asserting nationalistic superiority? Do they hear us as demeaning their faith or their faithfulness?

To what degree should we remember the remnant principle as we read 2 Chronicles 7:14? While the Old Testament has much to say to and for the faithful remnant, we know that ancient Israel, in the main, rejected God and was destroyed (2 Kgs 2:29–31, Ezra 9:5–9, Isa 10:20–27). We also know that God brought a remnant home.

Has there ever been a nation where the majority of the people stayed faithful to God over the long term?

When we read 2 Chronicles 7:14, are we tempted to wrongly think, "If we just return to God, then our nation won't face problems anymore?" John 16:1-4 clearly states the opposite. When we teach from the passage, have we unintentionally made it easy for the devil to invite others to believe one of his most popular lies, "If we just walk with God faithfully, life will be nothing but continual prosperity"?

We see 2 Chronicles 7:14 misapplied in two major ways that often come in tandem. The first is absolutizing: If we as God's people humble ourselves, pray, seek God, and repent, then God **will** grant our petition. There can be no possibility of exception. Support for this certainty is drawn from many passages (Prov 10:24; Mark 11:24; Luke 11:9-10; John 11:22, 14:13, 15:16 & 16:23). Perhaps Matthew 21:22 is the clearest of all: "And whatever you ask in prayer, you will receive, if you have faith."

No one possessed stronger faith than Jesus, but His passionate prayer in Gethsemane was not answered by deliverance from the cross (Matt 26:37-47). Of mere humans, we have the highest respect for Paul's faith, but his thrice-repeated petition for physical deliverance was not granted (2 Cor 12:7-10). There is no reason to doubt David's faith or sincerity in praying for the life of his son, but the baby did not recover (2 Sam 12:15-23).

To be blunt, God does not always grant the deliverance that we request, nor should He. We err grievously when we present a biblical teaching as absolute when Scripture teaches us that it is not. Many years ago in a CCU waiting room at, we heard a preacher tell the family of a critically ill infant, "I told God last night, 'This child will not die!' I told God because I had prayed to God for the life of this child. Your child will not die." The baby died that night. We continue to wonder how the family dealt with this errant and arrogant claim. God hears prayer and blesses, but He is never obligated to deliver on demand (Dan 3:16-18). The preacher's words to the hurting family were false. He erred by forgetting that we are never allowed to put words in God's mouth. We cannot rightly say more than God says.

The popular "understanding" of 2 Chronicles 7:14 is beautifully concise. When God commands and we obey, problems end; it's a simple as that. But it isn't; there's a huge gulf between simple and simplistic. While we cherish ever word of Scripture and greatly value faith, we recognize the wisdom of letting the whole of Scripture speak. We dare not choose selective hearing. Both humility and sound reasoning remind us of the modern proverb: for every complex issue there's an answer that's simple, easy, and wrong.

The second major error of application with 2 Chronicles 7:14 concerns assumptions about specificity. Many seem to assume that any crisis of the moment addressed with humility, prayer, seeking, and repentance will be averted or ended by God. The pandemic will stop. The hurricane won't make landfall. The bomb won't explode. The war won't begin. The business won't fail. The person we love won't die. God does not give us such specific knowledge. The Bible offers no such specific promise. It's exceedingly dangerous and damaging to assume otherwise. As much as we might prefer otherwise, our trials and challenges often serve a higher purpose (Job 42:1-6, Rom 5:1-5, Heb 12:1-11, 1 Pet 2:18-25).

Like the tragic and apparently harmful events in the life of Joseph—being hated by his brothers, being sold into slavery, being falsely accused and imprisoned, and being forgotten in prison for two extra years—in the moment we often do not see a higher purpose or the BIGGER plan (Gen 37–50). We struggle to see how Romans 8:28 applies. We so want God to make it better right now. We want both answers and relief; we strongly prefer the comfort of certainty. But God knows us—and our needs—better than we know ourselves. God far more often blesses us, not with the comfort of certainty, but with the comfort and challenge of faith (2 Cor 5:7).

In understanding any passage, context counts. In applying any passage, we need to ask God for wisdom (Jas 1:5, Ps 119:26–27). In study and in teaching, humility remains a vital virtue. We are wise to confess our struggles with 2 Chronicles 7:14 and to welcome help in understanding.

"And He Shall Direct Your Paths"

Trust in the Lord with all your heart, and do not lean on your own understanding. In all your ways acknowledge him, and he will make straight your paths. Proverbs 3:5-6

Does God still direct our paths? In this non-miraculous age, does God still guide His people? If He does, how does He guide us?

Some believers disavow any form of divine guidance. In their view, divine guidance is an illogical concept. In the first place, they ask, "If God guides, then what about free will? How can we consistently affirm the personal responsibility and accountability of each individual?" Others add, "If God guides, then why do bad things happen to good people? Why doesn't God keep them out of harm's way?" Others query, "If God guides, how does He guide? If you can't tell me how, then I can't believe it."

If God guides, how does He guide? He guides through His word (Ps 119:105-106). He guides through the advice or assistance of others (Acts 9:23-25 and 23:11-22). He guides through providence, opening and closing "doors" that may not even be visible to us (Rom 1:13). Only by looking back through the eyes of faith do we come to see that God must have had a hand in directing events. Admittedly, this is an attribution made in faith, and it is certainly not a claim that we know all the mechanisms that God uses to bless and protect us.

If God guides, then why do bad things happen to good people? Why doesn't God keep them out of harm's way? We have no idea why God allowed James to be executed but rescued Peter (Acts 12). We have no idea why God allowed righteous Uriah to be killed while adulterous David was spared. We don't know why their first child died, but David and Bathsheba lived. We have no idea why God allowed a lie to kill his servant in 1 Kings 13 while the prophet who told the lie was allowed to live. We don't know because God did not choose to reveal that information. He doesn't owe us an explanation. Some mysteries are beyond us. Perhaps they serve to remind us of our limitations. Dwelling on the mysteries rather than the facts of revelation seems futile.

If God guides, then what about free will? How can we consistently affirm the personal responsibility and accountability of each individual? The fact that God guides those who are willing to be guided does not imply that His guidance is overwhelming or irresistible. Obviously, it is possible to reject the will of God (Luke 7:30). It is possible to "quench the Spirit" (1 Thess 5:19). It is possible to reject the gospel and to fail to love the truth (2 Thess 1:8 and 2:11). It's possible, but it's deadly. God wants to direct our paths, but He does so only with our consent and cooperation.

Comfort and Grace

Blessed be the God and Father of our Lord Jesus Christ, the Father of mercies and God of all comfort, who comforts us in all our affliction, so that we may be able to comfort those who are in any affliction with the comfort with which we ourselves are comforted by God. 2 Corinthians 1:3–4

In the passage above, "affliction" refers first to persecution. But the truth of God's comfort extends to many circumstances. As the "God of all comfort," He is able to comfort us in countless ways. He offers comfort to the righteous in every situation.

God comforts through Scripture. Think of Psalm 23, John 14:1–5, Romans 8, 1 Corinthians 13, 1 Thessalonians 4:13–18, and Revelation 21:1–5 and 22:1–5. We have seen faithful families take courage in the reading of these passages during times of illness and death.

God comforts through prayer. For the faithful, God's listening ear and loving heart are most precious treasures. Think of Philippians 4:6–7. As we make our requests known to God with thanksgiving, He blesses us with peace and guards our hearts and minds. Think of 1 Peter 5:5–7. As we humble ourselves under God's mighty hand, He invites us to cast all our cares on Him.

God comforts through reflection. How many of the Psalms are

David's reflections on the goodness and deliverance of God? Psalm 27:13 reads, "I believe that I shall look upon the goodness of the Lord in the land of the living!" The next verse adds, "Wait on the Lord: Be strong, and let your heart take courage; wait for the Lord." We don't just wait; we contemplate, remember, and welcome God's help.

God comforts through writing. The Psalms blessed David just as they bless us. "Writing out" our pain is good, but writing in ways that honor God and comfort others is better.

God comforts through work, particularly through service to others. Think of Elijah in 1 Kings 19. Under Jezebel's threat, Elijah believed he was alone and hopeless. After God fed and encouraged him, He assigned Elijah a series of jobs. Involvement in God's work helped Elijah reconnect with life.

God comforts through people. Think of family, friends, and good-hearted strangers. Jesus comforted Mary and Martha even before He raised Lazarus (John 11). Jesus both took comfort from and offered comfort to the thief on the cross (Luke 23:39–43).

And God comforts to make us comforters. He gives so we can share His gifts. As surely as sorrows unite us in suffering, giving comfort unites us in grace.

Saved by Grace Through Faith

What then? Are we to sin because we are not under law but under grace? By no means! Romans 6:1

Paul knew what his critics would ask, so he—by inspiration—asked and answered first. "Doesn't teaching salvation by grace through faith encourage sin?" After all, Paul had written, "But where sin increased, grace abounded all the more" (Rom 5:20). He knew that some would read those words and charge, "To teach salvation by grace through faith is to be soft on sin!"

Paul's answer is unmistakable: "God forbid!" "May it never be so!" "By no means!" "Certainly not!" We easily grasp both his meaning and his intensity.

Salvation by the grace of God through faith in Jesus Christ is the very heart of the gospel. Its truth is essential and undeniable. It is the only way any sinner can be saved. And it is in no way "soft on sin."

Salvation by grace through faith involves nothing less than a death to sin. The Roman Christians knew that. They had been baptized into the death of Jesus, buried with Him, in order to die to sin. They were commanded by Paul, "So you also must consider yourselves dead to sin …" (Rom 6:11).

Salvation by grace through faith involves nothing less than a change of masters. Everyone who has been buried with Christ in baptism should "walk in newness of life" (Rom 6:4). Not only are such people dead to sin, we are also "alive to God in Christ Jesus" (Rom 6:11). We are no longer servants of sin. We have been freed to become servants of righteousness, grace, and God (Rom 6:13–16).

Salvation by grace through faith involves nothing less than a change of purpose. Christians can and should walk in newness of life (Rom 6:4). We should not obey the lusts/pleasures of sin (Rom 6:10, 12, 14). We are commanded to count ourselves dead to sin (Rom 6:11). We are commanded not to let sin reign in our bodies (Rom 6:12). We are commanded to yield ourselves to God (Rom 6:13, 22; Matt 6:24). After all, just like the Roman Christians, we have "become obedient from the heart to the standard of teaching to which you were committed" (Rom 6:17). Don't you love the reminder that when God's doctrine was delivered to us, we committed ourselves to God and His doctrine?

Salvation by grace through faith involves nothing less than a change of destiny. Serving sin always leads to death (Rom 6:23, Jas 1:13–15, Isa 59:1–2). Serving God leads to holiness, righteousness, and eternal life through Jesus Christ (Rom 6:7–10, 8:1).

"Soft on sin?" What an unfair and unfounded charge! Salvation by grace through faith involves nothing less than being reconciled to God by the death of His Son (Rom 5:1–2, 6:4–5 and 23). Salvation by grace through faith gives us every reason to live humbly, gratefully, reverently, righteously, and obediently before Him. It gives us every reason to love God with all our hearts and to seek to please Him in all things (Matt 22:37–38, Col 3:17 and 23–24).

Christians

Christians are imperfect people. We have sinned and still do. Yet, we don't live in sin, condone sin, or excuse sin. We have repented of our sins and have been cleansed by the precious blood of Jesus Christ (1 John 1:7-10, Acts 2:37-38).

Christians are obedient people. We realize the importance of God's commandments. We keep, value, and abide in the Word. We know that to do otherwise is to live a lie (1 John 2:3-6).

Christians are loving people. We know that to hate is to walk in darkness (1 John 2:8-11). We love not just "in word or talk but in deed and in truth" (1 John 3:18). We love because God is love, and God first loved us (1 John 4:7-21).

Christians are abiding people. We understand that abiding in Christ carries obligations. We want truth to abide in us because only those who know and do the will of God can abide forever. We abide in Him because of the promise of eternal life (John 8:31-32; 1 John 2:6, 17 and 24-25).

Christians are hopeful people. We believe that God has greater blessings in store than we have ever imagined. We hope to be fully like Jesus and to "see Him as He is" one day. In response to that hope, we work with God to purify ourselves and imitate Christ (1 John 3:1-3 and 5:11-13).

Christians are confident people. We walk with Crist so that our confidence will extend to the day of His return. Our confidence in

God exceeds our trust in ourselves both on the level of human emotions and of human reasoning. Our love for God overcomes our fears and brings us daily joy. God's promise and our faith makes us confident that our prayers are lovingly heard (1 John 2:28, 3:19–21, 4:17–18 and 5:14–15).

Euodia and Syntyche

I entreat Euodia and I entreat Syntyche to agree in the Lord. Philippians 4:2

I'm intrigued by Euodia and Syntyche. All we know of them is found in Philippians 4:2-3. They were Christian ladies who had worked with Paul for the sake of the gospel, but there was some issue between them.

I believe they illustrate the concept of purposeful ambiguity. We'd love to know what their conflict was, but Scripture doesn't tell us. It doesn't tell us because we don't need to know. By not knowing, we're invited to think, to explore, to question, and to recognize the limits of our knowledge. We're also invited to realize that the source of their conflict is not the issue. The fact of their conflict was the issue and the danger.

I feel for the "true companion" of Philippians 4:2, whom Paul urges to "help these women." What if they don't know that they need help? What if they don't want help? What if they're enjoying their conflict? What if each one has already recruited allies for the war? What if their positions are entrenched? What if both choose to hate Clement for meddling in their business?

Maybe I ask too many questions. I know that at least some of the questions flow from my constant "meddling" in the business of others. I intend to be helpful in the spirit of Matthew 7:12, 1

Corinthians 13, and Philippians 2:1–4, but I may not always fully know my own motives. I certainly don't always know how my attempts will be perceived by others.

In a stunningly joyful letter, Philippians 4:2–3 stands out as a rare non-positive comment. Why is it there? Why didn't Paul just let things lie? Consider the following:

- Unity has always been precious to God (Ps 133, John 17:21).
- The devil can use personal conflict to create great distraction and destruction.
- Things seldom fix themselves. "Ignore it, and it will go away" is usually a lie.

Conflict isn't always evil. It can be an opportunity for growth, focus, understanding, and communication. In this sin-damaged world, conflict is serious business. It can distract, discourage, and even destroy. It can rage, enrage, and escalate beyond all reason.

In any conflict, we're blessed to remember that God is always right. And only God is always right.

We're blessed to remember that honoring God is more important than meeting our needs in the moment. Selfishness can kill us and make us look terrible as it does.

We're blessed to remember that faithful servants of God can disagree. Like Paul and Barnabas in Acts 15:36–41, we can disagree in matters of judgment without either party being wrong.

We're blessed to remember that sometimes we win by losing. Sometimes we lose by winning. Given our limitations, we sometimes think we're winning when we're losing and vice-versa. Only God always knows. Wisdom demands that we avoid premature judgment.

We're blessed to remember that faith needs to trump feelings. Doing right matters more than feeling right. Right feelings often come long after right actions. We need to do the good that we know to do.

We're blessed to remember that we are called to be peacemakers, just like the "true companion" was (Matt 5:9, Rom 12:18, Phil 2:1–4).

To put it plainly, if we don't love our brethren, we don't love God (1 John 4:7–21). But as we love even the most challenging people, we both honor and imitate our Father in heaven.

Evil, Unbiblical, and Counterproductive

> *So Pilate entered his headquarters again and called Jesus and said to him, "Are you the King of the Jews?" Jesus answered, "Do you say this of your own accord, or did others say it to you about me?" Pilate answered, "Am I a Jew? Your own nation and the chief priests have delivered you over to me. What have you done?" Jesus answered, "My kingdom is not of this world. If my kingdom were of this world, my servants would have been fighting, that I might not be delivered over to the Jews. But my kingdom is not from the world."*
> *John 18:33–36*

It's evil, unbiblical, and counterproductive to attempt to convert anyone by force. Jesus called, taught, helped, served, challenged, confronted, and more, but He never forced a conversion. "Forced conversion" is an oxymoron. It's a logical impossibility. If spiritual conversion doesn't flow from a willing heart, it's not real.

As hard as it was, Jesus always respected a person's right to walk away. That's so clear in Mark 10. Jesus loved the rich young ruler. Loving him, Jesus told him the truth about his spiritual need. Loving him, Jesus let him walk away when he rejected the demands of discipleship.

The same is seen in Matthew 23:37–39. Jesus loved the people of

Jerusalem. He knew what they were doing to themselves by rejecting Him. And he respected their freedom to reject.

Jesus never taught His disciples to attack others. When physical violence was attempted to protect His life, Jesus stopped the sword and healed the damage then and there (Matt 26:51–56). The purpose of Jesus was never to destroy people's lives (John 3:16–21).

We find no joy when a mosque is bombed, a synagogue is vandalized, or a temple is attacked. We fight for men's minds, hearts, and souls. We fight with the weapons of love and truth for the good of all (Eph 6:10–20). We reject manipulation, compulsion, and deceit (2 Cor 4:2). We know that a tainted victory is no victory at all.

It's evil, unbiblical, and counterproductive to attack those who don't believe as we believe. Whether fire, bomb, gun, or threat, a Christian cannot rightly pursue personal vengeance (Rom 12:17–21). And the same can be said of lies and insults. Our mandate is to speak the truth in love as we overcome evil with good. We don't deny the presence or the power of evil. We don't call evil our friend. We oppose evil to the best of our ability. And we dare not use evil means in an attempt to promote or protect God's kingdom.

False Teachers

We know the dangers of false doctrine. Jesus described false prophets as "ravenous wolves" who deceitfully appear in sheep's clothing (Matt 7:15-20). Paul wrote of those who followed false doctrine as having departed from the faith as "devoting themselves to deceitful spirits and doctrines of demons" (1 Tim 4:1). Peter warned of those who twist Scripture itself "to their own destruction (2 Pet 1:14-18). Jesus Himself condemned the church in Pergamos for its toleration of false teachers (Rev 2:15-17).

We know the dangers of false doctrine, but do we remember that false doctrine involves more than just words? Of the false teachers mentioned in Matthew 7, Jesus said, "You will know them by their fruits" (Matt 7:16). "Their fruits" were more than just the results of their false teaching. "Their fruits" also included the behavior that accompanied their teaching.

The false teaching condemned in 1 Timothy 4:1 directly led to errant living. The behavioral component of twisting the Scriptures is clear in 2 Peter 3:14. Just as God wants all to "be diligent to be found by Him without spot or blemish, and in peace," the implication is that those who twist the Scriptures will not be found in that holy and safe condition. Revelation 2:12-17 also connects false teaching to false living. Those "who hold the teaching of Balaam" tempt their brethren to participate with idols and to commit sexual immorality. False teaching leads to false living, and the opposite is just as true.

The Bible is equally clear that false teaching can be done without words. 1 Timothy 1:8–11 lists several obvious sins, including striking one's parents, murder, sexual immorality, and lying. Notice the "catch all" phrase at the end of this list of sins—"and whatever else is contrary to sound doctrine" (1 Tim 1:10). Sin itself is contrary to sound doctrine. All sin is contrary to sound doctrine. False doctrine can be encouraged behaviorally; it can be encouraged and advanced through sinful living.

Titus 1:10–16 makes the same point. The language is strong. Paul cites a Cretan poet's unflattering description of his countrymen. By inspiration Paul says, "This testimony is true." Paul tells Titus what to do: "Therefore rebuke them sharply, that they may be sound in the faith" (Titus 1:13). The implication is clear: Their sinful behavior made them unsound. To make the point even stronger, notice Titus 1:16, "They profess to know God, but they deny him by their works."

Denying God is the ultimate false teaching. Whether done verbally or through ungodly living, it cannot be right or blessed. We are called to confess Christ and teach the truth with both our words and our lives. Our Lord deserves nothing less.

Conflicting Messages

When people see a conflict between words and actions, they're almost always going to believe what they see. That's one of the reasons the Bible gives such strong emphasis to consistency.

Matthew 7:21-23 stands as a classic example. Even the Lord believes what He sees. Using religious words and doing religious works is no substitute for genuine faithfulness. The danger of pick-and-choose religion is ancient. Many have chosen to do the things that cost little and to use the right religious words; but at the bottom line, they ignore God and do what they please.

Ancient priests led the people in this error. Think of Isaiah 1. The people brought their sacrifices and kept the appointed religious feasts, but they gave in to evil, oppressed the weak, and insulted God through their rebellion. Their worship and their lives were in direct conflict with God.

Luke 9 offers a piercing example. When a village of the Samaritans was rude to Jesus, James and John offered to call down fire like Elijah did in 1 Kings 18 and 2 Kings 1. Jesus allowed no conflicting message as He stoutly rejected their unkind offer. His message of hope remained untainted: "For God did not send his Son into the world to condemn the world, but in order that the world might be saved through him" (John 3:17).

Jesus condemned conflicting messages as He told of the Good Samaritan (Luke 10). The two religious figures in the story took no risk, made no effort, and showed no compassion. These two servants of God saw the urgent need of the moment, but both ignored it. By occupation, they could be identified as servants of God, but their lack of loving action denied Him (Titus 1:16).

Modern examples of conflicting messages amaze us. Weather reporters stand on the edge of the ocean in near gale force winds telling viewers to evacuate because of the unsafe conditions. If they really believed it to be so dangerous, would they be there? Are they immune to the elements? What should we believe, their words or their actions? Our ears or our eyes?

It's like the neighbor who exclaims his love for children but runs them off his lawn lest they damage his grass.

It's like the church member who prays for God to send seekers to worship but complains when those seekers sit in "his seat."

It's like the Christian who condemns gossip but proceeds to share the latest juicy tidbit.

It's like the Christian who teaches the class rightly condemning ungrateful, complaining Israel, but then imitates their negative approach to life as soon as class is over.

It's like singing "God Is Love" and then asserting that certain people just don't deserve love or forgiveness.

It's like quoting Acts 20:35 or 2 Corinthians 9:6-7 but never learning the joy of giving from the heart.

We're not immune. We need to be on guard. The danger of competing messages remains real. The devil uses such messages every day. We dare not assist him in obscuring God's truth.

"A Fool Gives Full Vent to His Spirit"

A fool gives full vent to his spirit, but a wise man quietly holds it back. Proverbs 29:11

We know it's important to guard our speech, but we also know that it isn't easy to practice. Sometimes our first thoughts aren't our best. Some thoughts should never be verbalized. Saying them will cost more than it could possibly pay.

The meal isn't the best. First thought might be, "Even the dog wouldn't eat this." But those are fighting words. Second might be, "This doesn't suit my palate." While it's better than "I didn't like it," it still sounds snooty. A better thought might be, "This was quite an interesting meal." It's open to several safe interpretations. Better still is, "I certainly appreciate the work you put into the meal tonight." It's complimentary. We can always appreciate effort, even if the outcome wasn't great.

"How do you like my new car?" First thought might be, "I'm jealous as I can be. Why do you have a new car when I don't?" That one needs to be followed by repentance and proper application of Romans 12:15. Second thought might be, "I'd never have chosen a convertible." True, but non-helpful. A better thought is, "I'm very happy for you. Tell me how you chose it." That one's affirming and can strengthen a friendship. It is always okay to think before speaking and to weigh the potential effects of our words.

"Would you like to go out to eat tonight?" First thought might be, "Only if the alternative is being attacked by wild dogs." Second might be, "If I have to." We never "have to." If we're willing to pay the price, we can refuse. A better thought would be, "If that would bless you, I'm for it." Better still is, "I'd love to spend the evening with you."

Suppose I asked you, "How did you like this article?" Your first thought might be, "I didn't know you could write." Second might be, "What article? It's too short and thin for that label" A kinder thought might be, "I'm glad you included Scripture in your writing. The word of the Lord always provides a blessing." If you have the time to listen, there's always, "Tell me what helped you decide to write about that." Today's answer would be, "I needed encouragement to swallow some bad thoughts and replace them with better ones. I needed to find a way NOT to play the fool." That answer may not be pretty or preferred, but it's true to life and to Proverbs 29:11.

Providence and Prayer

A family member was having trouble scheduling an important doctor's appointment. Finally, she secured one six weeks later. She thought to make the following request: "If you keep a cancellation list, put me on it. I'd love to come earlier." Within an hour she had an appointment on the next business day.

What do we make of such happenings? I think of several options. Some would blow it off under the general heading of "strange things happen." Oppositely, some would declare it a miracle from heaven. Others might chalk it up to karma—since she tends to be a good person and to treat people right, this appointment lined up for her.

We don't take any of those paths. Our thoughts turn to James 1:17, "Every good gift and every perfect gift is from above, coming down from the Father of lights, with whom there is no variation or shadow due to change." If it's a blessing, we choose to attribute it to God and His goodness. We admit that we don't know the mechanics or the details. We admit that we deserve no special treatment. We also admit that we're blessed to attribute good things to God.

How does attributing every good to God help us? We think of the following, but you are welcome to expand the list.

- It fits the tone and tenor of Scripture, including James 1:17 and Luke 11:9-13.
- It causes us to think of God. We are blessed to think of Him

in every moment (Phil 4:8).
- It encourages us toward gratitude (Phil 4:6–7).
- It lifts our spirits and improves our attitude.
- It helps us avoid the trap of self-congratulation: "This happened to us because we're good people who deserve such things."
- It motivates us to continue in prayer (Luke 18:1, 1 Thess 5:17).
- It helps us remember that God wants to shower His blessings on all of creation. He is far more able and more generous than we can imagine.
- It motivates us to be good to others, even the undeserving (Rom 12:14–21).

What if we're wrong? What if these apparent blessings are just happenstance, accidents of nature? Respect for truth would obligate us to change our thinking if such could be proven. Short of that, what's the negative in thinking of God, being grateful, avoiding pride, continuing in prayer, and remembering the goodness of our Creator? Can you see any downside here?

Our belief is that we will never know—at least in this life—all the ways that God blesses, helps, heals, protects and leads those who choose to follow Him. We will be stunningly impressed if God gives us this knowledge in the life to come. We don't even claim to fully grasp what Hebrews 1:14 says of angels: "Are they not all ministering spirits sent out to serve for the sake of those who are to inherit salvation?" Because we know some have entertained angels without realizing they were angels (Heb 13:2), doesn't it make sense that others have received help from angels without knowing who they were.

God is better than we know. We lack the capacity to grasp all the ways that He blesses us. Thankfully, we have the capacity to attribute all good to Him and to thank Him for His grace.

Love Abandoned

But I have this against you, that you have abandoned the love you had at first. Revelation 2:4

When Jesus looked at the church in Ephesus, He saw many strengths. The brethren toiled for His name's sake. They persevered and showed patience. They refused to compromise the doctrine of Christ, making sure that teachers stood firmly in the truth.

Despite these strengths, the church in Ephesus was in serious jeopardy. Unless they repented and returned to their first works, Jesus was going to extinguish their light. In what way or ways had they abandoned their initial love?

Some Bible students believe that the praise of Revelation 2:2–3 refers more to the earliest days of the church than to its condition at the time Jesus revealed His letter to John. While the church had a great beginning, had it become "weary of doing good" (Gal 6:9)? Had they left their first by resting on their laurels? Had they concluded, "We've done our share"?

Closely related, some Bible students believe that the praise of Revelation 2:2–3 refers to the current work of the church, but that the Ephesians' passion was waning. Were they forgetting that Jesus "gave himself for us, that He might redeem us from all lawlessness and purify for himself a people for his own possession, who are zealous for good works" (Titus 2:14)? Were they were losing their spiritual fire? Had someone convinced them that God-honoring works no longer mattered?

Some Bible students believe that the praise of Revelation 2:2-3 refers to the current work of the church, but that the brethren were losing the vital connection between what we do and why we do it. In terms of Matthew 6, were they acting to be seen of men rather than to bring glory to God? Were they missing the truth of Colossians 3:23, "Whatever you do, work heartily, as for the Lord and not for men, knowing that from the Lord you will receive the inheritance as your reward"? Is it that they weren't serving in the spirit of Christ?

Careful Bible students have observed that whatever abandoning their initial love involved, it clearly included the cessation of what Jesus called "the works you did at first" (Rev 2:5). Consider the following possibilities:

- Are they and we being reminded to revisit the earliest days of our discipleship and to get back to the basics of loving God and our neighbors (Matt 22:36-40)?
- Are we being reminded of our duty to care for others (Matt 25:31-46, Jas 2:14-17)?
- In that evangelism is not part of Jesus' commendation, some have suggested that the church in Ephesus was turning inward. Were the brethren working, showing patience, and opposing error, but no longer winning souls with urgency (Matt 28:18-20, Acts 8:4)?
- Were some of the brethren neglecting the precious opportunity to honor God and encourage one another by worshiping together (Heb 10:24-25)?

- Were some of the brethren failing to care for their own families (Eph 5:25–29, 1 Tim 5:8)?
- We love the Lord's brilliance in choosing NOT to describe "the love you had at first" or "the works you did at first." His divine restraint demands that we explore both concepts as broadly and biblically as possible. He invites us to examine our hearts, minds, and service.

At the same time, Revelation 2:1–7 also reminds us that a church—or a disciple—can be faithful in certain aspects but unfaithful in others. Faithfulness, even excellence, in select areas cannot excuse laxness in others. Jesus both demands and deserves our all (Rom 12:1–2).

Things Are Not Always as They Appear

For we know that if the tent that is our earthly home is destroyed, we have a building from God, a house not made with hands, eternal in the heavens.
2 Corinthians 5:1

Paul knew, even better than we do, that life can be grinding. When he wrote about the "God of all comfort, who comforts us in all our affliction, so that we may be able to comfort those who are in any affliction, with the comfort with which we ourselves are comforted by God" (2 Cor 1:3-4), he wrote as an expert. He didn't exaggerate when he wrote that "we share abundantly in Christ's sufferings" (2 Cor 1:5, 11:22-28). He realized that he and his coworkers were the very stench of death to those who were perishing (2 Cor 2:15-16). He knew that his physical body would perish (2 Cor 4:16).

Paul knew how all this would look to those who lack faith and spiritual perspective. He knew the questions they could ask. "What's the use? Why keep trying when everything seems to be against us? Why hold on to God and faith when trouble and death are inevitable?"

Paul knew the questions, but he also knew the answers! Things are not always as they appear. No matter how dark the day, no matter how difficult the challenge, no matter how deep the pain,

Paul could say to Christians:

- God Himself comforts His children (2 Cor 1:3–4).
- God's comfort enables and encourages us to comfort others (2 Cor 1:4).
- "… for we know that as you share in our sufferings, you will also share in our comfort" (2 Cor 1:7).
- God Himself makes us sufficient for the ministry to which He calls us (2 Cor 3:4–6).
- Knowing that God calls us through the gospel into His service, "we do not lose heart" (2 Cor 4:1, 16).

We do not lose heart because we belong to God. We do not lose heart because God renews us (2 Cor 4:16). We do not lose heart because we refuse to trust our limited human vision and our feeble human minds. Rather, we choose to look "to the things which are unseen" (2 Cor 4:18, 5:7). We do not lose heart because we trust God. He promises the faithful "an eternal weight of glory beyond all comparison" (2 Cor 4:17). No matter how things appear today, God will deliver abundantly and eternally!

Jesus Always Wins

The title of the blogpost did its job. I was hooked as soon as I saw "Jesus Always Wins." It triggered both my "Says who?" alarm and my bubblegum detector. It made me wonder, "How does this author define 'win'? Is his focus spiritual, psychological, or other?" It seems that I've always been a contrarian. Show me an assertion and I immediately want to test it. This one fails many times over.

"Jesus always wins," but Isaiah 53:3 correctly foretold, "He was despised and rejected by men, a man of sorrows and acquainted with grief, and as one from whom men hide their faces he was despised, and we esteemed him not." "He came to His own, and His own people did not receive Him" (John 1:11). "For not even His own brothers believed in him" (John 7:5). The people of His own region "took offense at Him" (Matt 13:57). The Samaritans of Luke 9:53 were among several groups who "did not receive Him" or asked Him to leave their region (Luke 8:37). Where's the win in Matthew 23:37–39?

"Jesus always wins," but "after this many of His disciples turned back and no longer walked with Him" (John 6:66). Jesus loved and taught the rich young ruler, but "disheartened by the saying, he went away sorrowful, for he had great possessions" (Mark 10:22). Jesus wanted the disciples to watch with Him and pray on the night of the betrayal, but three times He found them sleeping (Mark 14:32–42). After declaring, "Even though they all fall away, I will not" and being warned by Jesus, Peter denied the Lord three times (Mark 14:29–30 and 66–72). Judas betrayed Him with a kiss (Mark 14:43–45).

"Jesus always wins," but the stout warnings of Revelation 2:5, 2:16, 3:3, and 3:14–18 must be remembered. The Lord's church is not always faithful to Him. Some Christians choose to fall away, "crucifying once again the Son of God to their own harm and holding him up to contempt" (Heb 6:6). There are those who say "Lord, Lord," but do not know Him (Matt 7:21–23). There are those who "profess to know God, but they deny him by their works" (Titus 1:16).

"Jesus always wins" is worse than bubblegum. It's false, shallow, and misleading. It's too broad, non-nuanced, and too easily misunderstood. It sets Christians up for the equally false corollary, "Serve Jesus, and you will always win, too." That doesn't fit well with John 16:1–4, Acts 8:1–3, and 2 Corinthians 11:23–28. From a worldly perspective, no one always wins.

From a spiritual perspective, the difference is amazing. The ultimate victory of Jesus is both certain and absolute. He has already been given "the name that is above every name so that at the name of Jesus every knee should bow, in heaven and on earth and under the earth and every tongue should confess that Christ is Lord (Phil 2:9–11). Our Lord is the ultimate victor, and He shares His victory with the faithful. He shares that victory through His atoning death on the cross.

From a spiritual perspective, the difference is amazing on yet another level. God so often turns apparent or situational defeats into victories. Consider Romans 5:1–5 in light of Matthew 16:24–26, 19:30, and 20:16. What looks and feels like defeat is often the very opposite. Sacrifice and surrender lead to safety and salvation. Tribulations produce perseverance, which produces character, which brings hope.

Trusting in Jesus changes everything. Consider Romans 8:28 and 31–39; no ruler, power, or angel—not even death "will be able to separate us from the love of God that is in Christ Jesus our Lord." Now that's victory (1 Cor 15:51–58)! It's not that Jesus always wins; biblical truth is that Jesus has already won over sin, Satan, and death.

The Wrong Kind of Confession

We remember the late Jack Wilhelm saying, "The Lord never called us to confess other people's sins!" James 5:16 and 1 John 1:9 support his good statement. So do Ephesians 4:29 and 31.

I heard a lady say this in a local antique store on a Sunday afternoon: "I was too tired to go to church this morning. I really shouldn't be here." What's with that? Why offer confession to the store clerk? Why not choose to tell yourself the truth? We all know she was where she chose to be. To be blunt, she was where she wanted to be. And because she was violating her conscience, she couldn't even enjoy being there!

We've seen it in cartoons. A little boy gets caught red-handed and says to his mother, "I didn't do it, and besides I didn't mean to!" Pick one. Both untruth and inconsistency ruin confessions.

Think of a murderer who asserts, "Yes, I killed those three guys, but that's nothing compared to my partner. He killed four." Self-serving comparisons ruin any attempt at confession. The mega-evil of others doesn't make my evil less evil.

After he was caught, Adam confessed, but he first blamed Eve and accused God (Gen 3:12). He was 0 for 3 in his clumsy attempt. Genuine confession always works best if it's offered before we're backed into to a corner with no other choice. Confessions from the corner almost never work. They're incredibly hard to believe.

Think of King Saul's sad quasi-confession as he awaited a battle with the Philistines. He knew what he did was wrong, and he said to Samuel, "So I forced myself…" (1 Sam 13:12). He acted from fear and feelings rather than from faith. He knew it was wrong and did it anyway. Then he made things worse by failing to humble himself before God.

Some people confess like the one-talent man of Matthew 25:24, "Master I knew you to be a hard man, reaping where you did not sow, and gathering where you scattered no seed." That's a bit of insult at the beginning of an excuse. Insults and excuses always ruin confessions.

I remain perplexed by people who choose to make public confessions that begin, "If I have sinned…" I don't mean to be unkind, but please. We've all sinned (Rom 3:23, 1 John 1:8-10). Hedged confessions don't work either. They're the very opposite of penitent humility (2 Sam 12:13, Ps 51:3-4, Dan 9:3-11).

Dare we call the Pharisee's horrible words from Luke 18:11-12 a kind of twisted, sick confession? He chose to confess his virtues and his superiority in a way that was both ridiculous and repulsive. God has no respect for insincere confessions. And He always knows our hearts.

Evidences of Inspiration

We appreciate the classic evidences of biblical inspiration:

- the Bible's claim to be "breathed out by God" (2 Tim 3:14–17, 2 Pet 1:19–21).

- specific prophecies fulfilled, sometimes in the most unlikely of ways (Isa 53, Dan 7, Joel 2:28).

- internal coherence and congruence despite being penned by such diverse men over such a long time in diverse cultures.

- well-documented congruence between geographical and historical accounts of Scripture and discoveries from archeology, for example the existence of the Hittite nation.

- the power of Scripture to change lives.

We can also appreciate the lesser-emphasized evidences of divine inspiration.

The inclusion of challenging and difficult accounts that a mere human might well have chosen to omit. Think of the command to sacrifice Isaac (Gen 22) and the command to stop a plague by raising up a bronze serpent (Num 21). And Exodus 4:24–26 stands in a category all its own.

The inclusion of unlikely heroes, utterly counter to the prevailing culture. Think of Deborah the judge (Judg 4), Jael the heroine executioner (Judg 4), Huldah the prophetess (2 Chr 34), a tax collector and a zealot chosen as apostles (Matt 10:1–4), the Good Samaritan (Luke 10:25–37), and the Pharisees who warned Jesus (Luke 13:31).

The inclusion of dark episodes in the lives of heroes. Think of Abraham lying and laughing at God's promise (Gen 12:13, 17:17, 20:2). Think of David's adultery, deceit, and murder (2 Sam 11). Think of Peter's three-fold denial (Matt 26:69–75). Think of Barnabas, the consummate encourager, on one occasion becoming a discourager (Gal 2:13).

Descriptions of dark and heinous conduct without a hint of prurience. Think of Amnon's sin against Tamar (2 Sam 13). Think of the purposefully muted description of Jesus' sufferings before and on the cross (Isa 53, Matt 26–27).

The inclusion of utterly surprising accounts. Think of God showing mercy to King Ahab when he showed surprising humility (1 Kgs 21:29). Think of Esau the wronged hunter becoming a man of mercy and forgiveness (Gen 32). Think of God's grace to the Assyrians (Jonah).

The unapologetic accounts of God's judgment. Think of the ban on Canaanite nations (Deut 7:2, 13:15, 20:17). Think of

Uzzah and the ark (2 Sam 6). Think of the fierceness and finality of Matthew 7:21–24 and 24:48–50.

The uncompromising demand of faith in Jesus as the only Son of God (John 6:48–59, 8:24, 14:6; Acts 4:11–12) Think of the uncompromising clarity of John 15:1–8.

Jacob Wrestling with "God"

Metaphorically speaking, Jacob had been wrestling all his life. He struggled with Esau before their birth (Gen 25:22). He struggled to gain the birthright blessing (Gen 27). We hope he wrestled with his conscience as he deceived his own father. He struggled with Uncle Laban over his marriages to Laban's daughters (Gen 29). He lived in the middle of the struggle between Leah and Rachel (Gen 30, esp. v. 8). Genesis 31:36–42 documents his economic wrangling with Laban that eventually led to his move back home.

How fitting that a life filled with struggle features an all-night wrestling match on the eve of what he thinks will be his greatest contest to date, the homecoming battle with Esau and his 400 men.

Though Jacob believed that he had wrestled with God (Gen 32:30), we think of his opponent as an angel, a messenger from God (Gen 32:28). And we wonder why God initiated this encounter. Some scholars rightly remind us that God is always present—when we think Him absent, that's just poor thinking on our part. Others remind us that we wrestle with God whenever we attempt to ignore Him or to circumvent His will. Still others remind us that God wrestles with us because He loves us. He seeks our good; He seeks to save us from ourselves.

Some have suggested that Jacob's wrestling match is recorded to invite us to think about God and the struggles of life. We all have aspects of our past that are not pretty (Rom 3:23). All of us have been self-serving at times. All of us have been less than honest at times. All of us have let God, self, and family down. Deep in our hearts, our sins and flaws scare us. We know that sin bears cost (Rom 6:23, Isa 59:1–3). We know that we need God's help—we all need a major blessing.

We notice Jacob's perseverance in the midnight wrestling match; he refuses to give up even when his hip is damaged (Gen 32:25). He won't call the match a draw until he gets a blessing. And what blessing did he get? He gets a new name; no longer is he the supplanter; he is now the prince of God. He gets a reminder; he walks with a limp the rest of his life. And he gets a declaration of victory from the "man" whom he wrestled (Gen 32:28).

The "man's" declaration of Jacob's victory amazes me. In fairness, the match is a draw. Neither contestant defeats the other. Why is Jacob's opponent so generous with his words? He is God's messenger, and graciousness fills the heart of God. In addition, sometimes in the most challenging struggles of life, the height of victory is choosing to hold on, refusing to let go. Despite all his flaws, Jacob still trusts God's ability to bless. Jacob still trusts God's willingness to bless. He still understands something of how much he needs God's help.

I wouldn't assert that God will send an angel to wrestle with us in a physical contest. Yet I confidently assert that God still wrestles with us—should we say **for** us, on a regular basis. He makes the way of the transgressor difficult. He sends blessings to the faithful. He educates, encourages, and warns us through His word. He puts good people around us as examples. And He still has a way of handling our worst fears (Gen 33:4). No one ends a story like God!

Sin

Is any topic more politically incorrect than sin? Sin implies judgment, and even those who know nothing else about Scripture quote Matthew 7:1, "Judge not, that you be not judged." Of course, they almost always quote it in isolation, divorced from both its immediate context and the larger teaching of the Bible.

Modern people have little use for judgment because judgment implies a stable and understandable standard of belief and conduct. Judgment implies that knowledge exists and can be harnessed to guide human action. Judgment implies accountability. More and more, people seem willing to assert that each individual is accountable only to self.

In modern terms, sin and the judgment thereof is most often conceived as the arch enemy of love. Where love exists, judgment cannot. If God is love (1 John 1:8), then God doesn't judge. Judgment and the accompanying standards are devices created by those in power or who want power to limit and control others.

We know that modern thinking runs counter to Scripture time and again. Passages like Romans 11:22, "Note then the kindness and the severity of God …" and 2 Corinthians 5:10–11, "For we must all appear before the judgment seat of Christ, so that each one may receive what is due for what he has done in the body, whether good or evil. Therefore, knowing the fear of the Lord, we persuade others …" don't fit current preferences. The woes of Matthew 23 and the judgment parables of Matthew 25 are deemed unworthy of the Savior. But if there is no sin, why would anyone even need a Savior?

Lately, we're hearing more and more about the "need" to abandon concepts of truth, judgment, and morality as taught in the Bible. The Bible is presented as a flawed and contradictory product of mere human origin. Biblical doctrine is deemed divisive, condescending, and antiquated.

We know that even biblical doctrine can be presented insincerely, divisively, errantly, hypocritically, and condescendingly. There's nothing that can't be twisted and abused. The devil quoted Scripture to Jesus (Matt 4). Jesus recognized misuse of authority by religious leaders (Matt 23). Peter knew that some twisted Paul's teachings (2 Pet 3:14–18). But none of those abuses makes Scripture less true. The biblical mandate stands: "Do your best to present yourselves to God as one approved, a worker who has no need to be ashamed, rightly handling the word of truth" (2 Tim 2:15).

We love the truth of God. We love to live God's truth and to teach it—lovingly (Eph 4:15). We believe that truth leads us toward God and protects us from sin (Ps 119:9–11 and 105). Sin corrupts on so many levels. It'll make us think too highly of ourselves (Rom 12:3). It'll make us think that whatever we do is right (Prov 16:25 and 21:2). It will make us think that we're free to do as we please (Judg 17:6 and 21:25). It'll make us judge others by standards that we'd never apply to ourselves and feel secure while doing so (Matt 7:1–5).

Does God Still Punish Sin?

Yes, God still punishes sin, but maybe not in the ways that most people think. God has built the universe in such a manner that "The way of the treacherous is their ruin" (Prov 13:15). Much punishment is handled by what people commonly call cause and effect or natural consequences.

There's also self-punishment for sin in the form of guilt. Even the godly sorrow that works repentance hurts as it happens (2 Cor 7:8-12). Think also of David's pain over sin as documented in Psalm 51.

For believers, chastisement is a far more pertinent concept than punishment (Heb 12:1-11). God's goal is to grow us and protect us from ourselves.

The devil would have us believe that God is malicious, arbitrary, or some inexplicable combination. The devil would love for us to believe that God drops pain on people just because He can. We're much wiser to think of God in terms of 2 Corinthians 1:3-4 and 12:1-10. He is the God of all comfort. What may be a thorn from our perspective may be yet another gift that guards our souls.

That said, God is just and right to punish sin. He was right when He put Adam and Eve out of the garden and gave them other consequences. He was right when He banished Cain. He was right when He kept Moses out of the promised land. He was right when He let a faithless generation die in the wilderness. He was right when He let the men of Ai defeat His army after Achan's unfaithfulness.

As sad and heartrending as it was, God was right when He let David and Bathsheba's first son die. While we affirm the truth of Ezekiel 18, the sins of parents consistently affect and afflict their children. God was right when He let Israel fall to Assyria and Judah fall to Babylon. He was right when He allowed even His own temple to be plundered and destroyed.

As we move to the New Testament, God was right when He let Jerusalem fall to the Romans as foretold in Matthew 24. He was right when He took the lives of Ananias and Sapphira (Acts 5). He was right when He let His angel strike King Herod and take his life (Acts 12). God will be right and consistent when He keeps the fierce promise of Revelation 22:18–19. And God is right every time He fulfills the terrible promises of 2 Thessalonians 1:3–10 and upholds the teaching of Matthew 25:41–46.

We know that God's punishment of sin is not limited to the final judgment of humanity. Consider 2 Thessalonians 2:9–12. One of the strongest ways that God punishes sin is to let people believe the lies that they want to believe when they refuse to believe and love His truth.

We offer one HUGE caveat on this subject: Often people think God is punishing sin when that's not happening at all. Despite the accusations of his "friends," Job was not being punished for his sins. He was being attacked by the devil because of his faithfulness (Job 42:7–9). Naboth wasn't being punished for his sins. He was framed and murdered by an evil ruler (2 Kgs 21). Paul's thorn in the flesh wasn't a punishment for sin. Rather, it was an opportunity to rely on God's grace (2 Cor 12).

Imagine how the persecution of the church in Smyrna looked from a human point of view (Rev 2:8–11). What had they done to anger God? Why were they being punished? Jesus makes clear that their persecution was not from God. Jesus viewed them as rich, faithful, and precious brethren who were under fierce attack from Satan.

Jesus Himself rejected the false notion that every negative life event is God's judgment of sin as recorded in Luke 13:1–5. Jesus challenged the errant assumption of the people reporting to Him. He called them—and us—to see the tragedies and fragility of life as occasions for self-examination, repentance, and stronger recognition of our need to walk with God.

God Is Better at Forgiving Than We Are at Sinning

I know we must be careful with the title statement above. The devil would have us read it in an assortment of unbiblical ways. As it were, he'd sit on our shoulders and whisper in our ears, "Because God is so good, loving, and powerful, sin is nothing to fear. Just 'sin away' and leave forgiveness to God." "Because God loves to forgive, your sin is no big deal. Sin does no real harm. It just gives God all the more opportunity to shower you with grace." "Because God is so forgiving, sin can't doom or damage you. God will take care of it."

God is better at forgiving than we are at sinning, but sin still led to the universal flood (Gen 6–8). Iniquity still separates people from God (Isa 59:1–3). Sin still kills (Rom 3:23, Eph 2:1–3). It's stunningly unbiblical to minimize the effects of sin. Those who have died to sin must not continue to live in sin (Rom 6).

Despite the devil's lies and the HUGE costs of sin, we still affirm that God is better at forgiving than we are at sinning. The biblical evidence is abundant. Who but God could forgive His friend (Abraham) for lying and for laughing at His promise? Who but God could give His chosen people opportunity after opportunity to return to His favor and re-welcome His leadership (Judges)? Who but God could put away the sins of adultery and murder to keep His promise to a king (David)? Who but God would send His prophet to convict and redirect His wayward servant (David)?

From the New Testament, who but God would let a denier take the lead in preaching the gospel sermon on Pentecost (Peter)? Who but God would have the first post-resurrection gospel sermon preached to the very people who murdered His Son (Pentecost in Acts 2)? Who but God would confront and convert the chief persecutor of His church, commissioning that former persecutor as an apostle and a missionary (Paul)?

God has been, is, and forever shall be better at forgiving than we are at sinning. We have His word on it, and we delight in that truth. There's not a more beautiful paragraph in Scripture than Romans 5:6-11. And that great text does not stand alone. Think of Ephesians 2:1-10 and 1 John 1:5-2:2. We'd be blessed to read these three passages every day.

God is better at forgiving than we are at sinning. And that fact should never invite us to give in to sin. It should never invite us to presume on His grace. Rather, it should cause us to reject and battle sin with every fiber of our being (Rom 6:12-14).

God is better at forgiving sin than we are at sinning. That sweet truth should shield our hearts from the false guilt that Satan loves to promote (1 John 3:19-20). It should cause us to "draw near [to God] with a true heart in full assurance of faith…" because God remembers our sins no more if we are in Christ (Heb 10:16-25). It should cause us to serve God in joy as we owe Him our lives and our hope (Rom 5:6-8, Eph 2:1-10). And it should cause us to love God with all our heart, soul, mind, and strength (Mark 12:30).

Obeying the Gospel

"Just how does one 'obey the gospel'? 'Gospel' is good news. Good news of any kind is not obeyed. It is either believed and accepted or rejected—not obeyed."

As I read those words online, I realized that I've seen and heard them before. Such words both concern and sadden me.

We know that the gospel is good news, the best and most wondrous of all good news. It expresses the loving heart of the living God. It offers hope, redemption, restoration, reconciliation, and forgiveness.

It's amazing to me that some conclude that the gospel cannot be obeyed because it is good news. My mind doesn't work that way. More than that, even if my mind tended to work that way, I hope I would trust the word of God more than I trust my own thinking. Please consider the following.

"But they have not all **obeyed the gospel** ..." (Rom 10:16)

"... In flaming fire inflicting vengeance on those who do not know God, and on those who do not **obey the gospel** of our Lord Jesus Christ" (2 Thess 1:8)

"For it is time for judgment to begin at the household of

God, and if it begins with us, what will be the outcome for those who do not **obey the gospel** of God?" (1 Pet 4:17)

While thinking on those verses, we also remember 1 Peter 4:11: Whoever is blessed to speak for God, let him do so "as one who speaks oracles of God. ..." Always be faithful to God's truth. We can't improve on biblical language.

We know that scripture can be twisted (2 Pet 3:14–18). We know that scripture can be taken out of context and misused (Matt 4:6). We know that scripture can be heard but not obeyed (Jas 1:22–25). We should also know that it is never wrong to use a scriptural phrase in a scriptural way. If the Bible uses the phrase "obey the gospel," then we have neither reason nor standing to oppose the phrase. If our "logic" says otherwise, we have immediate need to check and correct our thinking.

I have strong desire to continue to urge all people to obey the gospel of Jesus Christ. Obeying the gospel pleases God and brings joy to the angels of heaven (Luke 15:7, Acts 8:35–39 and 16:30–34). Obeying the gospel is the path of grace and faith through which the Lord adds us to His church (Acts 2:41–47, Eph 2:1–10). Obeying the gospel allows God to move us from the domain of darkness into the kingdom of His dear Son (Col 1:13–14).

All this reminds me that I need to continually check my thinking. If a phrase or concept seems wrong, unhelpful, or misleading, I need to check it against scripture. If it's a biblical phrase rightly employed, then my thinking needs adjustment. That attitude and action would properly follow 1 Peter 5:6, "Humble yourselves, therefore, under the mighty hand of God so that at the proper time he may exalt you."

"And Do not Grieve the Holy Spirit of God"

And do not grieve the Holy Spirit of God by whom you were sealed for the day of redemption. Ephesians 4:30

We love the teachings and implications of Ephesians 4:30. At baptism, we receive "the gift of the Holy Spirit" (Acts 2:38). God, who has anointed and established every believer, "has also put his seal on us and given us his Spirit in our hearts as a guarantee" (2 Cor 1:22 and 5:5, Ephesians 1:13). The Spirit of God lives within every Christian.

The fact that the Spirit of God lives within every Christian does not remove our ability to choose our attitudes and actions. It does not remove our personal responsibility before God. Galatians 5:16–26 documents that so clearly. Paul urges Christians, "… walk by the Spirit, and you will not gratify the desires of the flesh," (Gal 5:16) and "If we live by the Spirit, let us also walk by the Spirit" (Gal 5:25). As long as we are in the body, there's an ongoing battle between the Spirit and the flesh.

There is nothing special about the word translated "grieve" in Ephesians 4:30. It's the same word for pain or distress that's used multiple times in 2 Corinthians 2 and 6:10. William Mounce helpfully writes, "Finally one use of *lypeo* serves as proof of the personality of the Holy Spirit, who is said to grieve at the sins of Christians." (*Mounce's Complete Expository Dictionary of Old &*

New Testament Words, 2006).

By faith Christians are to welcome the presence of the Holy Spirit. By Divine instruction, we are to choose to "walk in the Spirit." When we fail to "walk in the Spirit" by following the principles and precepts of Scripture, we oppose and disappoint the Holy Spirit of God.

The context of Ephesians 4 strongly supports these conclusions. Christians are reminded, "… you must no longer walk as the Gentiles do, in the futility of their minds" (Eph 4:17). Practicing impurity and greediness must be rejected (4:19). Having been taught the truth in Jesus (Eph 4:21), we actively "put off" the corrupt, darkened, and alienated "old self" (Eph 4:22), and we actively "put on the new self, created after the likeness of God, in true righteousness and holiness" (Eph 4:24).

With God's help, we choose to grow more and more like Christ (Eph 4:15). We reject theft, anger, bitterness, and corrupt talk (Eph 4:25–29) because embracing those sins would grieve the Holy Spirit of God.

What a wonderful warning and encouragement! God is helping us do right and grow in the image of His Son. He loves us and wants us to choose to trust and obey. As surely as sinful choices "grieve the Holy Spirit of God," God-honoring choices must bring Him great joy.

Righteousness and Peace

And a harvest of righteousness is sown in peace by those who make peace. James 3:18

There's much truth in the adage "He who defines the terms wins the debate." The devil knows this so well. He pushes people to define righteous as judgmental, condescending, and holier-than-thou. Of course, that's self-righteousness rather than biblical righteousness. It makes for pain, envy, and jealousy. It makes for war.

James 3:18 speaks of genuine righteousness, the kind that flows from heavenly wisdom. It's beautifully described in 3:18: "first pure, then peaceable, gentle, open to reason, full of mercy and good fruits, impartial and sincere." What a lovely set of virtues.

> Pure. Unmixed (Matt 5:8, Ps 15). Unadulterated. Genuine. Real. Not watered down.

> Peaceable. Loving peace. Seeking peace. Acting peaceably. Praying for peace (Matt 5:9, Rom 12:18 and 14:19).

> Gentle. Sweet. Caring. Loving. Never bullying. Entreating rather than demanding—think of Paul's sweet letter to Philemon. Recognizing its limitations and people's right to

choose, even if they choose poorly (Mark 10:21-22).

Open to reason. Willing to listen. Happy to learn. Willing to yield in matters of judgment. Not self-serving. Not self-seeking. Not self-promoting. Not demanding its rights. Not willing to "win" at the expense of truth or love (Rom 14).

Full of mercy. Merciful as a way of life. Overflowing with mercy. Abounding in mercy. Looking to God as the source and pattern of mercy (Matt 5:7, John 8:1-11).

Full of good fruits. Serving. Blessing. Bettering. So connected to God that good follows us and flows through us (Gal 5:22-26).

Impartial. Seeing everyone as a precious soul beloved of God and made in the image of God (Gen 1:26-27). Seeing all as needing the gospel. Seeing everyone as precious to God and sought by Jesus. Seeing everyone as worthy of respect and love—just because they are.

Without hypocrisy. Not posturing. Not faking. Not manipulating. As stated with "pure" above, both real and genuine (1 Cor 13:4-8, 1 Pet 5:5-11).

We love the description of God's reign as "a kingdom of right relationships." Just as James 3 emphasizes treating people right in word and deed, 1 John 4 emphasizes loving one another as God has loved us. "He who does not love, does not know love, for God is love." "Beloved, If God so loved us, we also ought to love one another." "He who does not love his brother whom he has seen, how can he love God whom he has not seen?"

The devil loves to mis-define the terms: "Don't emphasize righteousness and hold yourself accountable before God. That's evil and off-putting. That disrespects others and makes for conflict." God stands in truth: "Put on righteousness—real, biblical righteousness, and you will become an instrument of peace." What a joy to love, peace and make peace and sow pace!

"It Is More Blessed to Give"

And remember the words of the Lord Jesus, how he himself said, "It is more blessed to give than to receive."
Acts 20:35b

Logically, it is more blessed to give than to receive. In order to give, we must have been blessed with resources. Paul made that point to the Ephesian elders in Acts 20:35. One of the reasons that Paul urged others to work hard, just as he did, was that laboring allows us to "help the weak." We know that "weak" is a relative term. Compared to us and even to the Corinthian Christians of the first century, the Macedonians were stunningly poor. Paul wrote of their "severest affliction" and "extreme poverty" (2 Cor 8:2). But compared to their famine-stricken brethren in Judea, even they had something to give. Because they did, we do! Blessings equip us to give.

Developmentally, it is more blessed to give than to receive. Yes, there is a virtue in learning to receive a gift with gratitude and grace. But most agree that the grace of giving is harder to learn. In this sin-damaged and selfish world, the rule is "What's mine is mine, and I'm going to keep it." Though they had little material wealth, Jesus and the twelve carried money to help the poor (John 13:29). The first Christians gave sacrificially and distributed to all "as any had need" (Acts 2:44–45 and 4:34–37). Giving stretches the soul; it deepens the heart. Giving helps us walk in the steps and know the mind of Christ.

Relationally, it is more blessed to give than to receive. To give in love, we must first love. We must in some practical sense "in humility count others more significant than" ourselves (Phil 2:3). We must choose to "look out not only for [our] own interests, but also for the interests of others" (Phil 2:4). We must in some way allow His soul to be knit to the soul of those in need. Giving flows from love and builds love.

Spiritually, it is more blessed to give than to receive. Giving away hard-earned goods makes little sense from a material perspective. Giving away hard-earned goods with no expectation of repayment makes even less sense. From a spiritual perspective, Christians cannot do this; we cannot give without hope of repayment. On the surface this sounds like a contradiction of Luke 14:12–14 where Jesus commanded His disciples to offer dinner invitations to those who could not repay them. Upon reflection, it's exactly the point made by Jesus in this text. "And you will be blessed, because they cannot repay you; for you shall be repaid at the resurrection of the just." God will keep count and settle debts!

Eternally, it is more blessed to give than to receive. Things are just things, tools to be used to God's glory. Ownership is really stewardship; "For we brought nothing into the world, and we cannot take anything out of the world (1Tim 6:7). God's promise is "… whoever sows bountifully will also reap bountifully" (2 Cor 9:6). We keep only what we give. But when we give to God's glory, we keep and reap everlastingly.

Change for the Sake of Change, aka Fixing What Isn't Broken

Even when it's inconvenient, our better nature moves us to support change that makes life better. We might have loved the old "pours so slowly" ketchup bottles, but we see the superiority of the new "fast squeeze" version. Our Gmail at work recently moved to an improved format. It's one of the few software updates that I could immediately embrace. Younger drivers can't conceive of a time without power brakes, power steering, and blinkers that don't turn themselves off.

Some like change for the sake of change, even when it's just change. I think the cereal is the same whether it's Sugar Pops or Corn Pops, whether it's Sugar Smacks or Honey Smacks. The PR may be better, but the PR is all that's different. Whether Comcast or Xfinity, it was hard to talk to a human on the phone or to hide the grimace when someone says "customer service." Thankfully, there's been great improvement in recent years. The Caribbean remains the Caribbean, the same islands and sea, no matter how it is pronounced.

In all of life, especially concerning our service to God, we love the principle of 1 Thessalonians 4:9–12. Even when we're doing great, we want to "increase more and more." We don't object to good optics—looking right while we're doing right—but we want our growth to be more than cosmetic. We know that genuine growth is substantive (Eph 4:11–16, 2 Pet 1:5–8).

Change that's negative—"backwards progress"—is another matter. Several years ago, Our insurance agent, whose office was two minutes from our house retired. "For our convenience," the company changed us to an agent whose office was eight miles away. By the time I learn where the items are in a store, they rearrange everything "for my convenience." "When we all get to heaven" is not improved as "when the saved get to heaven." We never embraced universalism, and we were not being tempted to deny Matthew 7:13–14. We were the saved singing of our hope to the saved. We didn't need to fix what was neither broken nor about to break.

Several truths about change help me greatly. First, it's wise to welcome improvement, but to remember that truth can't be improved (Ps 119:89).

In a flawed and finite world, change is inevitable. Resistance to all forms of change is futile and unbiblical. That makes Hebrews 13:8 all the more impressive. Think of the precious line from the precious song, "O Thou who changest not, abide with me." God is the only constant, the only one we can always count on without reservation.

Sometimes it's not the fact of change that scares, angers, or grieves us. Sometimes our pain flows from the pace or means of change. Kindness, consideration, and communication will always matter (Phil 2:1–4, 2 Tim 3:23–26).

Never underestimate the power of tiny change. Negatively, few who leave God leave Him all at once. Far more drift away bit by bit (Heb 2:1–4). Positively, faith in God as a grain of mustard seed has limitless potential (Matt 17:20, Dan 2:44).

"Change" is a broad word. Change can be good, neutral, or bad. Change can be improvement, decline, or merely different wording or new packaging that is used to hide stagnation.

If It Ain't Broke...

We all know the adage, "If it ain't broke, don't fix it." It's bad grammar, but clear communication. Often, it's dead-on target. Some may remember the "New Coke" fiasco. Test tastes proved that people preferred it to the Classic Coke formula. But initially, the product failed miserably. The bottling company failed to recognize the human factor, the psychology of the change. People felt that something precious was being taken away from them. They snapped up the available supply of "real Coke." They complained with vigor. At least to some degree, the company relented and kept "real Coke" on the market.

We've seen similar situations with restaurants. For some inexplicable reason, they change the recipe of our favorite dishes. We see the same thing in stores. Just when we're comfortable and know where everything is, they rearrange everything "for our convenience." I'm told this is purposeful; moving everything causes us to hunt items. As we search for what we want, we notice, and presumably purchase, additional items. As a creature of habit, I love the usual, the familiar. In so many situations, "If it ain't broke, don't fix it" is an excellent action-guiding principle. But, there's another side to the story.

One of the rules back on the farm was to change the oil in every tractor after every 100 hours of operation—you use "hours of operation" to determine when maintenance is due. I've seen my folks leave the field in the middle of a job to honor that rule. Nothing was broken, but the life of the engine is in its maintenance. In the long run, they saved tons of time and money by faithfully following the maintenance schedule.

Similarly, relationships require maintenance. Relationships work best when they're continually improving. "If it ain't broke, don't fix it" is incompatible with numerous biblical passages. Consider 1 Thessalonians 4:9–10:

> Now concerning brotherly love you have no need for anyone to write to you, for you yourselves have been taught by God to love one another, for that indeed is what you are doing to all the brothers throughout Macedonia. But we urge you, brothers, to do this more and more.

Consider 2 Peter 1:12–13,

> Therefore I intend always to remind you of these qualities, though you know them and are established in the truth that you have. I think it is right, as long as I am in this body, to stir you up by way of reminder. ...

That very principle of seeking growth and improvement is the moving force behind 2 Peter 1:5–11 and Hebrews 5:11–6:3. As we give God our best today, He works in us and with us to "better our best" each day (Phil 2:12–13).

The devil is both devious and brilliant. If we're lazy, self-satisfied, or less than respectful of God's word, he'll tell us, "If it ain't broke, don't fix it. You're as good as any and better than most. Just keep the status quo and God will be happy enough." If we're willing to grow, he'll tell us, "Keep up with the times. Don't worry about the old ways or the old paths, even if God's word commands them. Just change as you think best." We need to recognize and resist his games.

Change

Change is a neutral word. It's neither the devil that some suppose nor the panacea that others embrace. It can be natural and wonderful—think of the daily growth of an infant. It can be natural and ugly—think of a favorite tree damaged by lightning and slowly losing its life. It can be unnatural and horrific—think of a nation falling into lawlessness or a person descending into addiction. Change can be God-honoring—the angels in heaven rejoice when a sinner repents (Luke 15:10). It can be God-rejecting—think of Paul's great accusation in Galatians 1:6 or his stunning denunciations in 2 Timothy 4:9–10 and 14.

In many respects, change is inevitable. It has been said that to live is to change. While this statement is not the whole truth, it accurately expresses an important truth. To oppose all change is futility. Worse, to oppose all change is to ignore God's truth. Children are meant to grow "in wisdom and in stature, and in favor with God and man" (Luke 2:52). As Christians, "we are to grow up in every way into him who is the head, into Christ" (Eph 4:15). God expects spiritual growth, which is, of course, positive spiritual change (Heb 5:12–6:3). Ongoing, positive change is mandated by 2 Peter 1:5–8. Psalm 55:19 condemns the disrespect of those who oppose God and reject repentance, saying, "… because they do not change, they do not fear God." Respecting God demands repentance.

In many respects, change is disconcerting. Many of us prefer the familiar. We love our comfort zones. We're tempted to oppose an unfamiliar hymn simply because it's new to us. We're tempted to oppose a change in the order of worship, even if that change is adding a prayer or a song before we extend the opportunity to give. While it's good to be careful, it's never good to be too careful. Our preferences never carry the weight of truth.

Those of us who love ritual and routine are wise to think lovingly of our brethren who value variety and freshness. A biblical sermon-in-song may be different, but it's clearly biblical (Eph 5:19, Col 3:16). An assembly that gives special emphasis to the Lord's Supper, prayer, thanksgiving, or the reading of the Word is just as biblical (1 Thess 5:15–18, 1 Tim 2:2–7). Different is not always bad.

On the other hand, there are things that do not and must not change. In explaining God's mercy toward Israel, Malachi 3:6 says, "For I the Lord do not change …" Hebrews 13:8 documents the changeless nature and character of Jesus Christ. Psalm 119:89–90 affirms, "Forever, O Lord, your word is firmly fixed in the heavens. Your faithfulness endures to all generations …" Proverbs 24:21 warns against even associating with those who are "given to" the wrong kind of change. Jeremiah 2:11 offers the ultimate warning against ungodly change, changing to "gods which are not gods." In light of these truths, to embrace all change is both thoughtless and unbiblical. Study! Think! Always trust God to lead us in the way of truth. Stay ready to change in any way that brings us closer to God.

Childlike or Childish

The comparisons below originated in a rich and happy Bible class discussion of Mark 10:13-16. Even as this book was being edited, additional ideas were suggested. We think of it as a work in progress awaiting the next happy insight and addition.

Obviously, there are ways in which we need to be like little children. Oppositely, 1 Corinthians 13:11 and Ephesians 4:11-16 remind us that there are ways we must NOT be childish. The following contrasts can help us hold these vital truths in biblical tension.

Children shine in purity of heart as they trust. They exude the beauty of innocence. But we know better than to be naïve, uncritically accepting every assertion that anyone makes (1 John 4:1).

Children love freely, honestly, and completely. If sin brings childishness, love of self brings envy, jealousy, and possessiveness.

Children love to learn. They learn eagerly and naturally. They find joy in the process of discovery. Childish people have been known to say, "Why are you making me learn this? I don't need to know this. I already know more than I can do."

Most children are born with a PhD in happiness. Think of listening to a group of children at play. The childish can't find true joy even when they get their way. Life never quite matches their expectations.

Children don't do stress. They nap when they need to nap. They often show amazing resilience and flexibility. The childlike would rather break than bend. They prize the rigidity of self-will.

Children acceptance their dependence. In their better moments, they both request and appreciate assistance. The childlike deny needing anyone for anything. On their worst days, they claim utter self-sufficiency.

Children are generous with their hugs and their effort. They love to help even with the task is bigger than they are. The childish weaponize or economize their assets. They can't share without first asking, "What's in this for me?"

Children are kind. Many of them sense pain and discouragement in others. When they do, they draw you a picture, offer to share a toy, or just need to sit with you. The childish disappear when they sense anything negative. They won't be bothered by the needs of others.

Children are amazingly accepting. Beauty and the Beast makes perfect sense to them. The beast is as the beast does, not as he might appear. The childish are too busy ridiculing the beast to notice the beauty of his heart.

Children are quick to make friends. Their default setting is "Hello, my name is Joey. We can be friends." The childish approach life from a different direction. "Can you be of use to me? How can you make my life better? If you can't, I'm done here."

Children are filled with a sense of wonder. A frog on the window or a dandelion flower amaze them. The childish want to squish the frog and reject the flower as a weed. They've lost the sense of amazement.

Children forgive with astounding simplicity. "That's okay. Let's play now." There's no concept of keeping score or holding grudges.

The childish count, record, replay, and worsen every wrong. Every "wrong" becomes an intentional attack that must be met with force. No wonder Jesus said, "Let the children come to me; do not hinder them, for to such belongs the kingdom of God. Truly, I say to you, whoever does not receive the kingdom of God like a child will not enter it" (Mark 10:14).

Some Things Require Too Much Faith to Believe

> *Now faith is the assurance of things hoped for, the conviction of things not seen. For by it the people of old received their commendation. By faith we understand that the universe was created by the word of God, so that what is seen was not made out of things that are visible...And without faith it is impossible to please him, for whoever would draw near to God must believe that he exists and that he rewards those who seek him. Hebrews 11:1–3 and 6*

We all know that nothing comes from nothing. It takes way too much faith to believe that the universe is self-creating. It takes almost as much faith to believe that matter and energy are eternal. Everything we know tells us that energy dissipates, that ordered systems tend to move toward disorder. Only an eternal, uncaused Creator is sufficient explanation for the origin of the universe.

We all know that life doesn't come from non-life. Modern biologists don't believe in abiogenesis, that living organisms arise from non-living matter—except for what must have happened in the beginning. According to evolutionary theory, life began from non-life. That theory allows no other choice "within the realm of science. [I know this isn't really within the realm of science, but science still claims it. Science claims it because the only alternative is divine creation—God.] Thus, the argument regarding abiogenesis is, "It happened then, but it doesn't happen now. It can't happen now because it's impossible. But it must have happened then because there's no other scientific explanation for the origin of life."

It takes way too much faith to believe that advanced forms of life are caused by a series of accidents. Advanced forms of life are too intricate, too complex. From the endocrine system to the nervous system, so much is intertwined and interdependent. How could natural selection "select for" hormones that support structures which cannot function without them? Can random mutations, pure chance, explain this? Within the sphere of Darwinian evolution, it must be the explanation. That takes too much "faith" for me.

So many brethren seem to be retreating from the biblical account of creation. Genesis is being labeled as myth, metaphor, or "accommodation to the pre-scientific thinking of primitive man." Jesus didn't retreat from the biblical account of creation (Matt 19:1–6). Paul didn't retreat from that account (Acts 17:24, Col 1:15–18). Neither should we. Some things are beyond scientific explanation. Some things belong to the realm of the spiritual. Some things make sense only through faith in the eternal, living God.

The Real Undead

Though it's no compliment to say so, on occasion I have watched a zombie movie. If you haven't, that is a compliment to you. Zombie movies are generally mindless. The "undead" pursue their foolish victims, often moving in slow motion. Despite their limitations, they tend to catch and eat most of them. A few zombies sometimes escape—in case there's a sequel. Most of it is silly drivel.

The undead are not, however, a myth. Their numbers are legion. Somehow they have missed the crucial promise of Jesus, "I came that they may have life, and have it abundantly" (John 10:10). They have missed the crucial power of Jesus: "I am the way, and the truth, and the life. No one comes to the Father except through Me" (John 14:6). They have missed the crucial prayer of Jesus, "Sanctify them in the truth; your word is truth" (John 17:17). Many of them have no clue that they are spiritually dead.

You know that I mean no insult to the spiritually dead. All of us were at one time among them. Ephesians 2 begins "And were dead in the trespasses and sins in which you once walked. …" That text speaks of Christians. It speaks of the power of God's grace, moving us from dead and condemned to alive and blessed. It invites us to remember where we were when God redeemed us.

Paul vividly describes the spiritual condition of all people before they came to Christ. Before being baptized into Christ, all accountable people come to live in "the futility of their minds" (Eph

4:17). They are "darkened in their understanding, alienated from the life of God ..." (Eph 4:18). They are callous and "corrupt through deceitful desires" (Eph 4: 23). While such people walk, talk, and function in the real world—many of them with remarkable kindness and intelligence, the biblical language above describes the spiritually dead.

Scripture calls us to see the spiritually dead as dead, not for the sake of judgment, gloating, or asserting superiority. Rather than condemnation, the primary mission of Jesus Christ was to bring and be God's offer of salvation (John 3:17). He told the truth about sin and its costs (John 8:24). He also told the truth about grace and its benefits (John 14:1-4). He was not willing to leave the dead without hope. If we are truly His disciples, neither can we.

Eternally Homeless

A deeply spiritual friend from another state kindly shared news of a nearby congregation's outstanding gift for disaster relief in Haiti. There wasn't a hint of jealousy in what she wrote. She knows how the Lord loves the poor and urges His people to care for them. She knows how helping the hurting can increase receptivity to the gospel. Given all that, I am still struck by her closing words:

> I guess the human part of us feels the pain of the disaster victims, and we can't help but give to help the starving and homeless. I wonder why people can't see that people are starving for the Gospel and will be eternally homeless.

My friend is compassionate. She and her family reach out to those with physical needs. She'd never do like the scribes and Pharisees in Matthew 15, declaring what might have been used to meet legitimate physical needs unavailable because it has been "dedicated" as a gift to God. She knows that people need food, clothing, and shelter.

On top of that, my friend has dedicated her life to world evangelism. She knows the truth of Luke 9:25: "For what does it profit a man if he gains the whole world, and loses or forfeits himself?" She knows the truth of Romans 1:16: "For I am not ashamed of the gospel, for it is the power of God for salvation to everyone who believes, for the Jew first and also for the Greek." She knows the truth of John 4:10: "If you knew the gift of God, and who it is that is saying to you, 'Give Me a drink,' you would have asked Him, and He would have given you living water." She knows the truth of 2 Corinthians 5:10–11,

> For we must all appear before the judgment seat of Christ, so that each one may receive what is due to him for what he has done in the body, whether good or evil. Therefore, knowing the fear of the Lord, we persuade others.

To feel compassion is one of the ways that we are made in the image of God. To show compassion is to follow the example of Jesus. Compassion is a wonderful virtue, but I understand my friend's point. It's stunningly easy to feel a greater sense of urgency over physical needs than spiritual needs. It's stunningly easy to help people physically without an accompanying plan to put the gospel before them. It's stunningly easy to forget that those who leave this world without Christ will be eternally homeless (Matt 7:21–23 and 25:41–46, John 8:24 and 14:6).

We reject the false dichotomy; it's not that we must choose to offer either physical help or spiritual help. It's not either bread or spiritual bread. It's not either clean water or living water. It's always been and will always be both. It's both in love and in faith. But it's both in biblical balance and with biblical priority. We help with physical needs as much as God allows, but the ultimate goal is always spiritual life. We work, pray, teach, and sacrifice to leave no one eternally homeless.

Where There's Smoke...

The sports world was abuzz with accusations of impropriety involving a Heisman Trophy candidate. And years later, I still don't have a clue which, if any, of those accusations were true. But tons of folks were passionately certain that they knew. People are amazing.

Some are sure of major impropriety just because of the volume and intensity of the accusations. Their mantra is, "Where there's smoke, there's fire." Even if there's often an element of truth in that secular proverb, it doesn't tell us when the fire started, who started it, why they started it, or who will be burned. Sometimes it's not "where there's smoke there's fire." Sometimes it turns out that where there's smoke, there's an evil group with a smoke machine.

Biblically, "Where there's smoke, there's fire" doesn't always hold true. In Acts 21 some supposed that Paul had brought Greeks into the temple and defiled that holy place. They had seen Paul with Greeks earlier. Then, they saw him in the temple with some fellow Jews. Paul's enemies added two and two and got six. And they moved to kill him based on this errant information.

In that same chapter, the Roman commander ordered Paul to be beaten. He knew Paul was in conflict in a Jewish city. Inexplicably, he thought Paul to be a disruptive Egyptian. It never occurred to him that Paul could be a Roman citizen. Assumptions can kill.

Jesus was accused of being a glutton and a drunkard because He was a friend of tax collectors and sinners (Matt 11:16–19). Even though He had explained His desire to call sinners to repentance (Matt 9:10–13), His enemies assumed that smoke always meant fire. And they thought they had observed a pattern of sin. They accused Him of blasphemy (Matt 9:3). Their line was "He casts out demons by the prince demons" (Matt 9:34). They accused Him of breaking the Sabbath and allowing His disciples to do likewise (Matt 12:1–14).

We all know that Jesus was condemned and crucified based on inconsistent false accusations (Mark 14:53–59) and a twisting of His own words (Luke 22:70–71). Never was a man the victim of so many assumptions and lies.

I'm so happy that we're not in the accusing business. Scripture invites us not to speak evil of people, but "to be submissive to rulers and authorities, to be obedient, to be ready for every good work" (Titus 3:1). Scripture commands us to "avoid foolish controversies, genealogies, dissensions, and quarrels about the law; for they are unprofitable and worthless" (Titus 3:9). Even when we must correct those who oppose God, we are reminded, "And the Lord's servant must not be quarrelsome, but kind to everyone, able to teach, patiently enduring evil, correcting his opponents with gentleness" (2 Tim 2:24–26). Our goal is always to help others "escape from the snare of the devil" and return to God's truth. The role of accuser isn't ours (Rev 12:10). Neither is it our task to believe or repeat every accusation we hear.

God's Freedom of Speech

Whoever keeps his mouth and his tongue keeps himself out of trouble. Proverbs 21:23

A fool gives full vent to his spirit, but a wise man quietly holds it back. Proverbs 29:11

A friend recently commented, "I'm noticing more and more people who have neither inside voices nor filters. They don't seem to give a thought to the fact that anyone around them can hear everything they're saying." I appreciate the insight. I wish I could argue with those facts.

There's a sense in which virtually everything we say should be "fit for human consumption." Our speech should "always be gracious, seasoned with salt …" (Col 4:6). We know the wisdom of Ephesians 4:29, "Let no corrupting talk proceed out of your mouths, but such as is good for building up, as fits the occasion, that it may give grace to those who hear." Our words should be so safe and loving that they would do no harm if they went record-making viral.

There's also a sense in which some things we say should be private, secure, and guarded. Some words are not meant for the public. Some words are true and important, but easily misunderstood. Some words are honest and biblical, but we need to wait for the best time and circumstance. Some words are sufficiently personal that they should be shared only among dear—and safe—friends.

Venting is greatly over-rated by some. "Just say what's on your mind, and let the chips fall where they may" isn't really as courageous as it sounds. That approach can be both selfish and destructive. Often our first thought isn't the best thought. Reflection and contemplation often bless us and those around us. Self-censoring can be nothing less than grace in action.

We love speech that offers grace. We love speech that encourages people toward Christ. We love speech that paves the way for healthy hearing of the gospel. Not only do we love such words, so does God.

It's different with the devil. He loves speech that titillates. He loves speech that tempts. He loves speech that distracts, damages, discourages, and destroys. He loves words that undermine faith and faithfulness. He loves speech that undermines the gospel and snatches the word out of our hearts. And if the devil can't get us to misuse our tongues, he will settle for making us timid and paranoid—so fearful of saying the wrong thing that we say nothing at all.

We love God's version of freedom of speech. We're free to encourage. We're free to warn. We're free to teach. We're free to use our tongues as instruments of grace, hope, peace, truth, and love. As we practice such positive, biblical communication, we'll be far too busy doing good to waste a single word in Satan's service.

The Delusions of Power

The delusions of power are myriad. They have ruined many people.

Think of Saul. When he was small in his own eyes (1 Sam 15:17), God elevated him to be king of Israel. When his attitude changed, he assumed power and prerogative that were not his (1 Sam 13:13 and 15:22–23). He learned that a crown isn't much without God's favor.

Think of Nabal in 1 Samuel 25. His possessions were in his power. No one could compel him to share. If he wanted to refuse hospitality, he could. But he could not do so and be right with God.

Think of David, the man after God's own heart. As king he had the power to take another man's wife. As king and commander, he had the power to take that man's life. But David lost control of his own children. Pain, violence, and embarrassment never left his house because he misused God-given power (2 Sam 11–24).

Think of Jezebel in 1 Kings 19. Even after the Lord granted Elijah victory over the 450 prophets of Baal and the 450 prophets of Asherah, she pronounced him as good as dead. Even in the face of a miracle of fire and a miracle of rain, she thought her power greater than God's.

Think of the parable of the foolish rich farmer. His economic power impressed him to the point of declaring, "Soul, you have ample goods laid up for many years; relax, eat, drink and be merry"

(Luke 12:19). It never occurred to him that you must stay alive to enjoy such good.

Think of the prodigal son (Luke 15). All he needed was freedom and funding. If only he had the power that money brings. He could run his life better without his father's guidance. He could enhance his joy if he were free to make his own decisions. But he ran his life into the ground.

Think of Pilate in John 19:10. He said to Jesus, "You will not speak to me? Do You not know that I have authority to release you and authority to crucify you?" Read verse 11 for Jesus' perfect response. Verses 12 and following make clear that Pilate was "played" by his Jewish subjects, moved to fear that caused him to do what he knew to be wrong.

Think of Herod in Acts 12. The people of Tyre and Sidon had little power, so they flattered the king to curry his favor. He controlled their food supply. As he "ate up" their flattery, he was eaten by worms and died. He had no clue of his mortality or of the ignominy of his death.

The delusions of power are myriad. People have long known this. Even common sense proverbs confirm it: Give a little man a little power and you'll make him smaller. Scripture tells us where real power resides. "Once God has spoken; twice have I heard this: that power belongs to God …" (Ps 62:11). "Great is our Lord, and abundant in power; his understanding is beyond measure" (Ps 147:5). He alone is great. All human power is incomplete, temporary, and derivative.

We Don't Know What We Don't Know

In preaching and in life, the statement holds true—we don't know what we don't know. Someone in the assembly seems distracted. Is he on a new medication, one with challenging side effects? Has she just learned of a family member's addiction? Was the latest medical test inconclusive with super scary possibilities left hanging? Is a job or a career in jeopardy? Or, am I just having a sub-par day as a preacher? Could I be totally misreading the situation?

We certainly don't know all the struggles being faced by the good people around us. We might not yet know the key new struggles being faced by those we count as close friends. If we're speaking specifically of me, I don't always know who counts me as a close friend—choices, criteria and definitions vary broadly. I've been quite surprised at different times—in both directions.

Given the fact of our limited knowledge and perception, several choices seem wise. Assume the best of people. Since we don't know what we don't know, don't make a negative judgment until evidence demands it.

Ask people how they are doing, and take the time to listen well. If they tell you, thank them for their trust, and pray for them BIG TIME. If they can't tell you, respect their silence, and pray for them even BIGGER. Not being told can be a great kindness.

Be a bright spot in whatever way God offers. When you see anything positive, say something positive. Be like Paul: compliment and encourage anything that shows faith, love, or hope (1 Thess 1:2–10). Tell people you are thankful to God for them. And be sure to thank God for them. Tell people that you love them, and make sure that you do (John 13:34–35, 1 Pet 4:8, 1 John 4:7).

When people are surly, remember that they may be bearing more load than we see. Remember that we may be neither the cause nor the target of their surliness. People in pain often aren't on their best behavior.

When people are awkward or ill at ease, don't write them off as inept or unloving. Not only is it true that none of us is always at our best, all of us are works in progress. We can learn and grow. We learn and grow best when people we respect cut us some slack and don't give up on us. Think of Jesus' patience with Peter. Think of God's patience with you.

Because we do not know what we do not know, it's wise and blessed to live the virtue of humility. Within biblical limits, an open mind is sweet. An open heart is even sweeter.

Because we do not know what we do not know, we should know something of how much we need the God who always knows, always loves, and always understands. He can help us protect our minds through the North Star of His truth. He can help us protect our hearts through the gospel of His grace.

We have no illusion that we'll one day know everything. That's beyond our grasp. But it's not beyond us to know God at a level that creates awe, love, and respect. It's within our grasp to hunger and thirst for an even deeper knowledge of Him (Matt 5:6, Phil 3:7–11). There's such peace in knowing that God knows—and knowing that we know Him.

Will My Life Matter?

Satan's cruelty is stunning! Even though he knows that selfishness destroys, he tempted even Jesus to act selfishly (Matt 4:3). Even though he knows that God is utterly good, he tempted even Jesus to presume upon the goodness of the Father (Matt 4:5–7). Even though he knows that "the law of the Lord is perfect ..., the testimony of the Lord is sure ..., the precepts of the Lord are right ..., and the commandments of the Lord are pure," he tempted even Jesus to misunderstand and misapply God's law (Ps 19:7-11). Knowing that "the heavens will pass away with a roar, and the heavenly bodies will be burned up and dissolved ...," he tempted even Jesus to choose fame and fortune over loyalty to God (2 Pet 3:10, Matt 4:8–9).

The devil loves to offer shortcuts to significance. He loves to offer substitutes that have the appearance of value, but hold no worth at all. He offers hollow dreams to hurting people, hoping that they'll trust their wishes more than they trust God's truth.

The devil loves to whisper lies. Through one means or another, he says to God's people, "You don't count. What's one among billions? Does anybody who matters even know who you are? Are you so arrogant as to think that your life really matters?"

The Lord loves to shout truth. We matter enough that He sent His Son to redeem us (John 3:16). We matter enough that Jesus Christ lets us wear His name (Acts 11:26). We matter enough that no power, whether physical, social, economic, political, or spiritual, "shall be able to separate us from the love of God which is in Christ Jesus our Lord" (Rom 8:35–39). Unless we rebel, we stand secure in Christ. We matter enough that God has entrusted the gospel to our care, as "God's fellow workers" (Matt 28:18–20, 1 Cor 3:9). We matter enough that God Himself intends to dwell with us forever (Rev 21:1–3).

Will my life matter? It will if it is lived in Christ. Not a single deed done to the glory of God will be forgotten (Matt 10:42, Heb 6:10). God will be glorified by every good work that we do in His name (Matt 5:16). God will be pleased by both our good deeds and our worship (Heb 13:15–16).

Will my life matter? It will if I help even one person obey the gospel of Christ or return to God's way of truth (Jas 5:19–20). To seek and save the lost is to step into the very mission of Jesus (Luke 19:10). Nothing, not even the whole material world, matters more than a soul (Matt 16:25–27)!

Did He Really Say That?

For we all stumble in many ways. And if anyone does not stumble in what he says, he is a perfect man, able also to bridle his whole body. James 3:2

I was listening to a basketball game as I worked. The commentator captured my attention most negatively when he said of a player, "And when he catches the ball in the paint with his hands…" How else would he catch the ball? With his feet? In his mouth?

I cringe every time I hear a college football announcer utter the worthless phrase "young freshman." Virtually all freshmen are young. It's noteworthy only when a freshman isn't young. The same goes for "young rookie" in professional ball.

With apologies to bikers, I was part of a conversation with a gentleman who fit the stereotype. From the scars to the body art, he was on the well-worn side of life. The subject of drug abuse came up. He denied any involvement. To reinforce the denial, he said of himself, "You can't look like this and do drugs." I was (and still am) thinking just the opposite.

Some counseling friends and I were in a training session in Atlanta. Regrettably, our presenter used salty language. But she began an even saltier quote of one of her clients with, "I don't curse." To make it even more ironic, around her neck she was wearing a cross on a chain.

I recently heard of a man who used a quintessential racist word in a text. When challenged by a friend, his reply was the classic "I'm not racist. I have black friends." The very use of the word is racist. Having 10,000 friends wouldn't change that.

I read from 3 John 2 in a recent sermon. Not once or twice, but three times, I caught myself saying, "As the Apostle Paul wrote…" I know Paul didn't write the book of 3 John. I have no clue why I wanted to credit the book to him.

What a challenge to get our language right! Factually right. Compassionately right. Non-redundantly right. Graciously right.

We know that it's a battle worth fighting. Redundancies and little slips of the tongue might merely be annoying. Untruth, hateful speech, and all unrighteous words aren't merely annoying. Such words deny the faith, obscure the gospel, dishonor the Lord, and endanger our souls.

> I tell you, on the day of judgment people will give account for every careless word they speak, for by your words you will be justified, and by your words you will be condemned (Matt 12:36–37).

We have God's word on that!

Honesty Remains the Best Policy

If free is unavailable, I like cheap. Target had the cheapest prices on colas that week. As we checked out, I asked Laura to check the receipt for accuracy. We were charged the advertised price on the colas, but there was a mistake. The scanner failed to record her shampoo. I waited in the truck as she returned to pay.

There was no temptation to steal the shampoo. Our consciences are too well trained. We'd have felt guilty because we would have been guilty. From Exodus 20 to Ephesians 4:28, it's clear that stealing is wrong. Doing wrong always damages the soul.

As we paid the first time with a debit card, Laura asked for $40 cash back. The clerk handed her two twenties. When she paid for the shampoo, Laura used one of those twenties. To her amusement, the clerk authenticated the bill with his "bill checker" pen. Laura told him, "I noticed you didn't check that twenty when you gave it me, but now you're checking it as I give it back." The irony zipped right over his head. Besides, he was just following store policy. I'm fine with following good policy.

Any time we refuse to steal, we've followed many sound policies. You could add notably to the following list:

- Matthew 5:6, "Blessed are those who hunger and thirst for righteousness, for they shall be satisfied."
- Matthew 5:13, "You are the salt of the earth, but if salt loses

its taste, how shall its saltiness be restored? It is no longer good for anything except to be thrown out and trampled under people's feet."
- Matthew 7:12, "So whatever you wish that others do to you, do also to them, for this is the Law and the Prophets."
- Ephesians 5:17, "Therefore do not be foolish, but understand what the will of the Lord is."
- 1 Peter 1:15, "…But as He who called you is holy, you also be holy in all your conduct…"

I'd hate to suffer spiritual defeat over a $6 bottle of shampoo. Doing right always pays in the long run.

No Good Deed …

You know how the devil completes that line. He and those deceived by him consistently repeat, "No good deed goes unpunished." And sometimes it seems like the devil is right.

A godly wife does all she can to live the truth of 1 Peter 3:1–6, but her husband doesn't respond with love. He intensifies his cruelty and rebellion to God.

Godly parents do all they can to live the truth of Proverbs 22:6 and Ephesians 6:4, but their children neither appreciate nor internalize that godly training. They choose self-will over wisdom and love.

Godly elders attempt to live up to the truth of Hebrews 13:17, but some brethren see them as meddlesome and overbearing. "Why can't they lighten up and join the modern world?"

Godly Christians do their best to apply Matthew 18:15–17 and Galatians 6:1–2, but they are accused of being self-righteous and judgmental. And Matthew 7:1–5 is cited as evidence.

Faithful Christians take to heart the Great Commission of Matthew 28:18–20, but they are accused of trying to force their religion on others. "After all, won't everyone eventually be saved anyway?"

Sadly, all this happens. Even stouter examples could be added. And Satan gloats when he persuades someone that righteousness costs far more than it pays.

Happily, Scripture countermands each of the devil's lies. It's just not true that "no good deed goes unpunished." Rather, in this sin-damaged world, it's more accurate to say that "few good deeds go unchallenged." Satan opposes good, especially good that's done in the name of Christ. Why? Because the devil knows the power of good deeds! Because the devil knows that good deeds honor God, help people, and mold Christian character.

What the devil opposes, God commends. In God's divine grace and mercy, for the faithful we can say, "No good deed goes unnoticed," "No good deed goes unappreciated," and "No good deed goes unrewarded." We have God's word on these truths.

Remember Matthew 25:31–46? Those who fed the hungry, gave drink to the thirsty, took in the stranger, clothed the naked, cared for the sick, and visited the prisoner heard these words from the King: "Truly, I say to you, as you did it to one of the least of these my brothers, you did it to me" (Matt 25:40). Remember Titus 3:8, where "those who have believed in God" are encouraged and empowered "to devote themselves good works." These things are good and profitable to men.

Remember Hebrews 6:10, "For God is not unjust so as to overlook your work and the love that you have shown for his name, in serving the saints as you still do." We have God's word on it. Love the Lord and no good deed goes unrewarded, but a caveat is in order. No good deed done righteously to the glory of God goes unnoticed, unappreciated, or unrewarded. But that doesn't mean that the reward will always be obvious, immediate, or earthly. And upon reflection, that's amazingly encouraging.

Even in this life, God often rewards better than we have any right to expect. Scripture offers many examples. In return for helping the spies escape, Rahab asked that her family be spared (Josh 2:8–14).

Not only was her family spared, but she became the great-grandmother of King David (Matt 1:5–6). On top of that, she's listed in the Honor Roll of Faith (Heb 11:31).

In return for great faithfulness, Caleb asked for the portion of Canaan where the giants lived (Josh 15:6–15). Joshua 15:11 tells us that his strength and eyesight were unabated by age. We'd never argue that these facts are unrelated.

David wanted to build a house for God (2 Sam 7). Though God didn't allow that, He rewarded David with these words, "Your throne shall be established forever" (2 Sam 7:16). What an acknowledgement of a good intention! On top of that, He let David's son build the temple that David had proposed.

Solomon chose wisdom when offered opportunity to request a gift from God (1 Kgs 3). Because his request pleased the Lord and showed humility, God gave him wisdom, riches, and honor above everyone on earth (1 Kgs 3:13).

An unnamed widow chose to give her all, two tiny coins, to God (Mark 12:41–44). For her act of faith, she lives forever as a shining example of trust and good will.

A woman anointed Jesus with costly fragrant oil (Mark 14:3–9). For her act of faith, "Wherever the gospel is preached in the whole world, what this woman has done will also be told as a memorial to her." What amazing return on an investment!

In the earliest days of the church, Barnabas sold land and brought the money to the apostles for the common good (Acts 4:36–37). God rewarded him with a role in helping Saul "plug into" the church in both Jerusalem and Antioch (Acts 9:26–27 and 11:25–26). The Holy Spirit chose Barnabas to lead the first divinely called mission team (Acts 13:1–3).

It can't rise to the level of Scripture, but it's a fine exercise to think of ways that God has already rewarded us for good works done in His name. And the best is yet to come!

Too _____ to Die?

And now I am about to go the way of all the earth. ...
Joshua 23:14

For the living know that they will die. ..." Ecclesiastes 9:5

... It is appointed for man to die once. ... Hebrews 9:27

People say it in jest all the time: "He'll outlive us all; he's too mean, too stubborn, too tough, too rich, too poor, too nice, too important, too talented, too useless, too ignorant, too slow, or too busy to die." The older among us may remember the line from the Tennessee Ernie Ford song, "Saint Peter, don't you call 'cause I can't go. I owe my soul to the company store." Sometimes it's even said that a person is too young to die. We should know better.

People may surprise us with their toughness or longevity, but everybody dies. And that need not be a morbid thought. Psalm 90:7–12 takes a different view of mortality: "So teach us to number our days, that we may get a heart of wisdom." We all know James 4:14–15, "... Yet you do not know what tomorrow will bring. For what is your life? For you are a mist that appears for a little time and then vanishes. Instead you ought to say, 'If the Lord wills, we shall live and do this or that.'"

Honestly facing mortality is healthy, mature, and biblical. It gives each day—each moment—value and uniqueness. It invites us to appreciate the special people who bless our lives. It urges us to hold on to God and to live each day in His favor.

My favorite science fiction characters are the Klingons. Their battle mantra is, "Today is a good day to die." In a serious and peaceful sense, Christians can claim that mantra. It's what Paul says in Philippians 1:19–26: "For to me to live is Christ, and to die is gain." In either case, Christ is magnified by our faithfulness. Being with Christ is key.

Except for those who remain until the coming of the Lord, all will die. We're wise to face this truth. We have the opportunity, the duty, and the choice to die prepared, ready to meet the Lord. And we all know that the only way to die ready is to live ready.

"I Was Only Joking"

Like a madman who throws firebrands, arrows, and death, is the man who deceives his neighbor and says, "I am only joking!" Proverbs 26:18–19

Perhaps you heard of the Australian radio personalities who, some years ago, impersonated Queen Elizabeth and Prince Charles as they called a London hospital to inquire about the health of the Duchess of York. When I heard the recording, even I thought that anyone would recognize them as fakes. But a nurse didn't and she gave them a bit of information that should have remained private. Tragically, a few days later the nurse took her own life.

The radio show was cancelled. I presume that the radio personalities were then unemployed. Their careers may have ended. To their credit, they issued tearful apologies explaining that they meant no harm and never expected the prank to go so far. I believed them. There's not a hint of a reason to believe that they thought this prank would have such tragic consequences. But they are forever linked to those consequences.

This brings to mind the famous statement of Deuteronomy 10:13 about the commandments and statutes of the Lord "which I am commanding you today for your good." We are so blessed to be protected by the wisdom of God as we keep His word.

We never know how fragile another person might be, but we

won't be tempted to press that person if we follow Matthew 7:12, Matthew 22:39-40, Ephesians 4:29, and Philippians 2:3-4. Each of those passages would protect us from exposing another person to danger.

We never know when a "joke" based in deception will backfire, but we know Ephesians 4:25, "Therefore, putting away lying, 'Let each one of you speak truth with his neighbor,' for we are members of one another." We know this was written to Christians about the treatment of fellow Christians, but we also know that we shouldn't lie—period.

We love good humor—humor that doesn't endanger others, humor that doesn't diminish others. We hate evil humor—humor that causes pain, stress, or embarrassment; humor that opens doors for the devil. God has always known both the danger and the difference. How blessed we are to access and appreciate His wisdom!

Live Dumb!

Trust in the Lord with all your heart and lean not on your own understanding. In all your ways acknowledge him, and he will make straight your paths. Do not be wise in your own eyes; fear the Lord and turn away from evil. It will be healing to your flesh and refreshment to your bones. Proverbs 3:5–8

Many reject the wise man's inspired counsel. They choose to chart their own path regardless of the consequences. To play devil's advocate, we offer the following advice for those who want to live dumb.

To live dumb, doubt everything and everyone. Become the consummate skeptic. Never trust anyone or anything. Avoid statements like "I know whom I have believed, and am convinced that he is able to guard until that Day what has been entrusted to me …" (2 Tim 1:12). Avoid statements like Paul makes in Colossians 4:7–15 where he lists fellow workers by name and calls them "beloved brother," "faithful minister," and "fellow servant." Never think of others as competent or diligent.

To live dumb, always question authority. Resent being limited by rules and laws. Do your best to ignore them. Inspire others to ignore them. Resist passages like 1 Corinthians 16:15–16 where Paul describes the faithfulness of those who devote themselves to ministry and says, "... be subject to such as these, and to every fellow worker and laborer." Don't even think about reading Hebrews 13:7 and 13 as they use BAD WORDS like leaders, remember, follow, obey, and submit. Forget Matthew 28:18, "All authority in heaven and on earth has been given me. ..."

Consistently assert your personal superiority. Think of yourself as the brightest and the best. Being prideful didn't permanently hurt King Nebuchadnezzar, not even his absence from the palace during the grass-eating phase (Dan 4). Pride didn't really kill King Herod; he eventually would have died anyway (Acts 12).

Use people. That's what they're here for. Deny that they're made in the image of God as Genesis 1:26–27 asserts. Deny that loving your neighbor as yourself isn't actually the second greatest command (Matt 22:39). Avoid Philippians 2:1–4. Sheep were made to be shorn and eaten.

Close your mind to new information. You already know more than you can do. Ignore that stuff in 2 Peter 1:5–7, "... Make every effort to supplement your faith virtue, and virtue with knowledge. ..." Ignore all those "grow in the grace and knowledge of the Lord Jesus Christ" passages. Ignore the example of Apollos with Aquila and Priscilla in Acts 18. No one really needs to learn the way of God more fully or more accurately.

Poke people whenever the opportunity presents itself. Be sure to poke family first and most. But never let anyone do the same to you. After all, "Love is patient and kind" is in 1 Corinthians 13, and you know the Corinthians had a boatload of problems. Don't think of Jesus as "gentle and lowly in heart" or of the meek inheriting the earth (Matt 5:5 and 11:28–30). Don't subject yourself to the Golden Rule. If you'd see hard times here and fall in the judgment, live dumb.

Things I Can't Wrap My Mind Around

I don't have a clue how many things qualify for this list. The items below aren't exhaustive; they are just some of the many that challenge me.

I can't imagine how The Right Reverend Apostle and Prophet John Doe could ever do a sermon from 1 Peter 5:5-7 or James 4:7-10. Only God is terrible and awesome. And no one on earth today meets the apostolic requirement of Acts 1:15-26. When it comes to labels and titles, there's nothing higher than Christian.

I can't comprehend how some Christians can be so negative and accusatory toward political leaders with whom they disagree in light of Romans 13 and 1 Timothy 2:1-7. Recognizing their imperfections, we can still pray for those who lead us. Never compromising biblical truth, we can still speak and act with civility and respect. Paul showed respect even toward those who broke the law in harming him (Acts 23:1-5).

I can't understand how individuals, families, or governments believe that they can spend more than they have or earn and remain solvent. I love the biblical virtue of self-control (Gal 5:22-23, 2 Pet 1:5-11, Prov 16:32 and 25:28). 1 Timothy 6 is stunningly clear on the blessings, limitations, and proper usage of money.

I can't fathom the thinking of parents who say, "I love my children too much to discipline them. I could never bear to disappoint them." Proverbs 23:13-14 urges parents, "Do not withhold discipline from a child," because loving, godly correction protects a child's soul. Proverbs 13:24 bluntly says, "He who spares his rod hates his son, but he who loves him is diligent to discipline him." Abuse is always wrong—even the abuse of apathy or permissiveness.

I can't understand those who say, "If I think it, I say it. I'm no hypocrite." Proverbs 29:11 begs to differ: "A fool gives full vent to his spirit, but a wise man holds it back." Some things should not be said. Other things should be said very carefully after much prayer. Practicing maturity and showing love are never hypocritical.

I can't believe those who say, "I couldn't help it. The pressure was too great. The temptation was too strong." That's not what we read in 1 Corinthians 10:12-13. God urges us to think, to rely on his faithfulness, to look for His way of escape, and to resist the devil steadfastly (1 Peter 5:8-9).

Everything scripture warns against is bad for us. When I choose any path other than God's path, I have chosen wrongly to my harm. And I should never try to wrap my limited mind around the assertion that I know better than God.

Wisdom

But the wisdom from above is first pure, then peaceable, gentle, open to reason, full of mercy and good fruits, impartial and sincere. James 3:17

The beginning of wisdom is this: Get wisdom, and whatever you do, get insight. Proverbs 4:7

Wisdom thinks before talking, leaves the harmful unsaid, and speaks the needed word (Prov 18:13, 29:20, and 29:11; Eph 4:29).

Wisdom thinks before acting, leaves the wrong undone, and accomplishes much good (Gen 39:1-9, Prov 22:3, Heb 11:24-26).

Wisdom thinks before—during and after—feeling, leaves the bitterness unfelt, and radiates love (2 Sam 18:5 and 30, Prov 20:22 and 25:21-22, Luke 15:17-24 and 23:34).

Wisdom thinks before believing, leaves the lie unbelieved, and loves truth (Gen 3:1-8, Deut 13:1-5, 1 Kgs 13:11-22, Prov 5:1-6 and 14:15, 1 John 4:1).

Wisdom thinks before accusing, leaves good hearts uncondemned, and admits its own frailties (1 Sam 17:28–29, Isa 6:1–5, Acts 21:26–29).

Wisdom thinks before demanding, leaves many orders unspoken, and simply asks instead (Matt 5:5, 6:9–13, 7:7–12, and 20:20–28; 1 Cor 13:4–5).

Wisdom thinks before striking back, leaves the personal slight in God's hands, and does good to all (2 Sam 16:5–13, Rom 12:17–21, 1 Cor 6:1–7).

Wisdom thinks before taking credit, leaves pride unaccepted, and gives God the glory (2 Sam 1:1–16, Luke 12:16–21, Acts 12:20–25).

Wisdom thinks before sinning, leaves momentary lusts unsatisfied, and pleases the God of heaven (Gen 39:1–9, Rom 3:23, Isa 59:1–2).

Wisdom thinks before deciding, leaves the mistakes of haste unmade, and proceeds with confidence (Josh 24:14–15, Prov 21:5, Isa 1:18–20).

Wisdom thinks before promising, leaves lesser tasks undone, and gives its best to God (Judg 11:29–31, Prov 20:25, Luke 9:57–62 and 14:25–28).

Wisdom thinks before forgetting, leaves no lesson unlearned, and grows all the wiser (Rom 15:4, 1 Cor 10:1–13, Phil 3:1–14).

Wisdom thinks of others before self, leaves ego behind, and

always thinks of God first (Lev 19:18, Matt 22:34–49, John 8:29, Phil 2:1–4).

Choosing an Attitude

It's clear in Philippians 4:4–9. We can choose joy, gentleness, and thanksgiving. When we do, the peace of God will guard our hearts and minds through Christ Jesus. This truth is amplified by the fact that Paul penned these words from prison.

It's just as clear in Colossians 3:12–17. We can choose mercy, kindness, humility, meekness, longsuffering, and love. When we do, we invite the peace of God to rule in our hearts, and we invite the word of Christ to dwell in us richly.

It's even clearer in Acts 5:41, where the apostles "left the presence of the council, rejoicing that they were counted worthy to suffer dishonor for the name." It's so powerful in Acts 7:60, where a dying Steven prayed for his killers, "Lord, do not hold this sin against them." It's most powerful in Luke 23:34, where Jesus prayed from the cross, "Father, forgive them, for they know not what they do."

In every circumstance or situation, we have the God-given ability to choose our attitude. In every circumstance or situation, we have the God-given opportunity to choose our attitude and our actions. In every circumstance or situation, we have the God-given responsibility to choose our attitude, our actions, and our words.

Once I lost a book of checks. I remembered taking them from the storage desk and moving them to the working desk in the den. My memory was exactly half right. Rather than getting angry with myself, I decided to do a bit of housecleaning as I searched. I found several things that I didn't even know were lost.

Uncharacteristically, I finally gave up the search and went to bed. The next morning, the checks were in the bed with me. I had laid them on the blanket when I took them from storage, and they were happy to stay there.

One Saturday, I took lemonade and fruit salad to the church building for the Sunday potluck. On the way, a car stopped short in front of me. The salad bowl tipped, and I lost a bit of juice. Rather than stewing over this—as I have been known to do, I managed to look on the brighter side. It was Saturday, and I wasn't in my Sunday clothes. I had more discretionary time for cleanup. The floor mat could dry overnight. I was in my truck rather than spilling sticky stuff in Laura's car. I lost only a bit of juice rather than the whole salad.

It's amazing how often little things trip us up. Tiny errors can ruin whole days or damage precious relationships. It's even more amazing how we can reframe apparent setbacks, looking for the good rather than dwelling on the inconvenience. We're blessed to put events in context and realize how minor many setbacks are. And even when losses are great, our God is greater. His blessings always outweigh our challenges. Even if that's not apparent on earth, we believe with all our hearts that it will be so in heaven.

Reframing

From now on, therefore, we regard no one according to the flesh. Even though we once regarded Christ according to the flesh, we regard him thus no longer. 2 Corinthians 5:16

Do not be conformed to the world, but be transformed by the renewal of your mind, that you may discern what is the will of God, what is good and acceptable and perfect. Romans 12:2

God knew about reframing before the word was coined. God has always known both the limitations and the possibilities of human thinking. We can get stuck in an errant perspective. Stubbornness, laziness, or ignorance can leave us trapped in bad thinking. But on our better days, we don't stay stuck. Thoughtfulness, humility, and the word of God move us to think, re-think, and grow.

On the bad days, people seem purposefully dense and aggravating. It's as if they choose to peeve us. Our first thought might be, "Oh no, not again. Why does this have to happen to me?" On our better days, we reframe. We choose to think from a spiritual perspective. We try to imitate the attitude of Christ.

While some might choose to grieve us, most people don't give us that much thought. I think of the most recent driver who turned across us on the four-lane; she wasn't attacking us. Perhaps she underestimated the distance or our speed. Perhaps she doesn't see well. Perhaps she wanted a new car and thought the first step was to kill the old one. Maybe she's always been a terrible driver. Whatever the case, she didn't even know us.

My first thought was to take offense. She could have killed us. We could have killed her. I've never wanted a new car enough to wreck an old one. Upon reflection, thank the Lord that the old car has good brakes. Thank the Lord we noticed her poor driving before we got too close. Thank the Lord we missed her. I can even thank the Lord that in this case, she was the bad driver and I was the good one. It's not like I haven't made the very same error. No need to blame or scold. No need to take personal offence. Reframe biblically. Find the blessing. Find and learn the lesson. Choose to think with kindness.

Biblical reframing isn't changing or ignoring facts. Rather, it's checking our perception and response. Are we thinking and acting maturely? Are we following and exhibiting the spirit of Christ? Are we being slaves to selfish habits and worldly patterns? Are we treating others as we'd have them treat us? Are we choosing to treat others better than they deserve, just like God has treated us? Are we letting God make us better?

Better Than We Deserve

It can be amazingly difficult to maintain a spiritual perspective when one of life's storms surrounds us. When things don't go as expected, we tend to lower our vision, to take our eyes off the goodness of God. Think of the ancient Israelites during the Exodus. When they got thirsty, hungry, or scared, they went so far as to accuse Moses—and by extension, God—of trying to murder them (Exod 14:10-12 and 16:1-3).

When life brings disappointment, we tend to look for external causation—who is doing this to me and why are they doing it? When life brings pain, we tend to focus on that pain. If we're not careful, we will begin either to miss or to minimize the blessings that God keeps sending us. If we're not vigilant and prayerful, everything will begin to look dark, and we will develop a terrible case of the "why me's."

One of the reasons we respect Paul so highly is that he kept his faith and perspective during the hard times. He chose to worship when beaten and bound in prison (Acts 16:25). He chose to see God's purpose in and God's deliverance from his sufferings (2 Cor 11:22-33). He chose to learn and to relish the sufficiency of God's grace (2 Cor 12:7-10). He chose to emphasize and to appreciate his ultimate victory through Christ (2 Tim 4:6-8).

For all of us, life is far better than we deserve. One reason we tend to "over notice" the bumps is that life is usually smoother than we realize. Most people around us tend to treat us well, offer help as needed, and forgive our errors. God keeps educating us and reminding us how much we need Him. Fellow Christians pray for us and offer encouragement with amazing consistency. Opportunities to serve God continue to abound.

Challenges come. Sometimes they come because of our sin and shortsightedness. Sometimes they come because we're trying to do right in a sin-damaged world. Every time we get to repent, God is treating us better than we deserve. And if we ever "do good and suffer," we still get treated better than we deserve. We get to follow the example of Christ, reaffirm our faith in Him, and remember how much He has endured for us (1 Pet 2:18–25).

What lessons should we draw from these truths? How should our experience of God's grace make us live?

- We who have received great grace should show great grace toward others (Matt 18:21–35).
- We who have been forgiven so much should freely forgive others (Eph 4:32).
- We who have been given such tremendous hope should offer God's hope to others (Acts 8:4).
- We who live as children of the Lord should thrive in joy and victory (Phil 4:4–10).

We for whom God has done such wondrous work should serve Him with purpose and passion (Titus 2:11–14). We should never let a complaint pass our lips (Phil 2:14).

Positive Enabling

We often hear about the negative side of enabling. There's a huge literature of codependency that warns against making it easy for people to continue self-destructive behavior. The dangers are acute, pervasive, and legendary.

Positive enabling is a blessed concept. Some describe it as setting people up for success. There's a wonderful example in 1 Chronicles 22.

David accepted God's decision that he would not be allowed to build the temple (1 Chr 22:7-8). Though God owed no explanation, He graciously provided one. David was a man of war. The temple of God would be built by a man of peace.

David chose to welcome the fact that his son would be allowed to build God's temple (22:9-10). No jealously. No bitterness. No competition. No complaint. No argument. David recognized and accepted God's blessing.

David chose to help his son in every way that he could, and he found many ways.

- He appointed skilled masons to hew stones (1 Chr 22:1).
- He prepared iron, bronze, and wood for the construction (1 Chr 22:3-4).
- He directly charged Solomon to build an excellent house for the Lord (1 Chr 22:5-6).

- He asked God to give his son wisdom and understanding (1 Chr 22:12).
- He reminded Solomon that God's favor depended on Solomon's faithfulness (1 Chr 22:12).
- He commanded the leaders and the workmen to help Solomon (1 Chr 22:17–18).
- He reminded everyone of God's gift of peace and rest (1 Chr 22:18).
- He urged all to serve by setting their hearts and souls to seek the Lord (1 Chr 22:19).

David set Solomon up for success. He positively enabled his son. He recognized that Solomon's task was great. He knew that Solomon was young and inexperienced (1 Chr 22:5). Without undermining or demeaning, David took practical steps to bless his son.

David sets a strong example for us. When others are doing right to the glory of God, we're blessed to bless them. As we encourage and contribute to their good works, we maximize God's blessing for all. What a joy to set our hearts and souls to seek the Lord and to build one another up in the name of the Lord!

Consistency

I'm never quite sure how to phrase it: is it that I love consistency or that I hate inconsistency?

My brother once had a tractor that would not behave consistently. Its electrical issue was intermittent—it acted up only when it wanted to. He'd take it to the shop, but he knew what would happen. It would never mess up while the mechanic was watching.

On the positive side, we love a restaurant that's consistent. A given dish comes out the same every time. The price is uniform. The service is always friendly. If I have to ask, "Is the salmon good today?" I have already admitted defeat.

We love Hebrews 13:8: "Jesus Christ is the same yesterday and today and forever." It's the perfect affirmation of consistency. Lest we miss that point, the very next verse urges us to be consistent in our faith, "strengthened by grace" and not "led away by diverse and strange teachings."

There are many ways we can show consistency in Christ.

- We can worship consistently with faith and passion (Heb 10:24–25 and 13:15).
- We can consistently show God's love to others (Heb 13:16, Gal 6:10).
- We can consistently value and add to our knowledge of God's word (Acts 17:11, 2 Tim 2:15).

- We can consistently do good works that bring glory to God (Matt 5:16, Titus 3:1).
- We can consistently show respect for God's authority (Col 3:17, 1 Pet 5:6).
- We can consistently encourage good works and good people (Eph 4:29, Gal 6:6).
- We can consistently pray for God's will to be honored (1 Thess 5:17, 1 Tim 2:1–4).
- We can consistently confess our sins and seek God's forgiveness (1 John 2:1–2, Jas 5:16).
- We can consistently "give all diligence" to grow in Christ (2 Pet 1:5–8 and 12–13).
- We can consistently "esteem others better" than ourselves and "look out for … the interests of others" (Phil 2:3–4).

Using Scripture to add to this list could fill weeks of happy Bible study. The amazing gracious and loving consistency of our God urges us to spiritual consistency. Ephesians 4:11–16 beautifully states our goal. We want to be fully and completely like Christ.

The Irony of Inconsistency I

Two friends and I attended a highly specialized seminar dealing with child custody assessment. Much of the material was excellent. We left with a huge folder of information and an increased awareness of a regrettable, but necessary, process. However, we also learned some other lessons.

The presenter was an expert in the field. He holds a terminal degree. His list of publications is impressive. His experience is extensive. And he's just as human as the rest of us.

Though he urged us to be on time for every session, not a single session started on time. Though he warned us against taking a condescending or adversarial stance in our work, he took a condescending stance toward one of the participants. He insulted the gentleman's question and repeated the insult several times. Though he encouraged us to be consummately professional in our work, during the seminar he was less than professional in attire, demeanor, and language.

Consistency is a rare jewel. We love it when we see it. It gives us assurance, comfort, and encouragement. It speaks of stability and soundness. More than that, it's a quality lived to perfection by Jesus. Brethren have long noted Luke's purpose in penning the gospel, to offer an account dealing "with all that Jesus began **to do and teach**" (Acts 1:1).

Inconsistency frustrates us. It raises doubts and reduces respect.

Whether in ourselves or in others, we know it should not be. Inconsistency frustrates and confuses us. It erodes confidence and trust. More than that, inconsistency is a quality strongly condemned by Jesus. In Matthew 23:2, Jesus acknowledged: "The scribes and the Pharisees sit on Moses' seat, so practice and observe whatever they tell you—but not what they do, for they preach but do not practice."

James 3:1–12 challenges sins of the tongue on the basis of inconsistency. "From the same mouth proceed blessing and cursing. My brothers, these things ought not to be so. Does a spring pour forth from the same opening both fresh and salt water? Can a fig tree, my brothers, bear olives, or a grapevine produce figs?"

Most of us are stunningly skilled at observing the inconsistencies of others. Most of us are far less skilled at recognizing and correcting our own inconsistencies. That's where faith and maturity enter the equation. Faith leads us to God's word for sound information and guidance. Faith and maturity lead us to our knees, seeking God's forgiveness and help. Anything that I hate when I see it in others is dead wrong in my life as well. No excuses. No denials. There's no substitute for genuine growth.

The Irony of Inconsistency II

And He who sent Me is with Me. The Father has not left Me alone, for I always do those things that please Him. John 8:29

Did you notice the word "always"? Jesus Christ lived with perfect consistency. His loyalty to the Father never wavered. His obedience was flawless. His love was perfect. We find such consistency both astounding and impressive.

Some suggest that we are "hardwired" to appreciate consistency. Others note how troubling we find inconsistency. Examples abound.

- A governor who won election on a platform of cleaning up corruption resigns amid embarrassing scandal.
- A candidate's aide contradicts his platform, or worse, secretly contributes to his opponent.
- "Professional wrestlers" try to tear one another apart, but party together after the match.
- A religious leader preaches morality but practices the opposite.

Comedians love such things. These errors provide fodder for countless jokes. Even those who see no humor in these matters feel a sense of distain, especially toward those who fall after claiming to promote ethics and morality. They hold those who claim to be moral to a higher standard.

As Christians, we heartily embrace that higher standard. While recognizing the truth of our imperfection (Rom 3, Eph 2:5), we gladly "hunger and thirst for righteousness" (Matt 5:6). We seek to be pure in heart and in action because we want to see and dwell with God (Ps 15, Matt 5:8).

All can fail. All can fall. All who have reached responsible status have fallen. Having fallen, it is so easy for us to excuse ourselves. It is so easy to do comparative analysis—"at least I'm not as bad as ___." But we know that Christian analysis is just the opposite.

For Christians, it always starts with Christ and stays with Christ. We seek to be like our Lord. We strive toward "the unity of the faith and of the knowledge of the Son of God, to mature manhood, to the measure of the stature of the fullness of Christ" (Eph 4:13). In humility, we know we have not arrived. In faith, we know that God works to bring us ever nearer to His heart (Phil 2:12–13).

Consistency and Grace

Back in the day, there were newspaper machines just outside the gift shop nearest the admissions office at Johns Hopkins Hospital. *The Baltimore Sun* was 75 cents from the machine; but you could buy one inside for $1.00 (for the math impaired?). *The Washington Post* was 75 cents inside but $1.00 from the machine. I was reminded—again—of how much I appreciate consistency.

One morning I chose pancakes for breakfast in the hospital cafeteria. The lady ahead of me made the same choice, but she rejected the first pancake offered to her. "I don't want that one, it's too small." I told the server that I wanted the three pancakes remaining on the tray, and I wasn't picky about the size. As I paid, the cashier charged me for only two. One of the three looked small to him. It reminds me of how much I appreciate grace. It more than made up for the money that the newspaper machine had eaten the day before.

I like the comfort of consistency, whenever it works to my good. I love to be surprised by gracious acts for the same reason. Both brighten the day.

I'm working to become more consistent and comforting to others in the manner of Romans 12:6–21, 1 Corinthians 15:58, Ephesians 4:29–32, Philippians 2:1–4, Titus 2:11–3:8, and 1 Peter 4:7–11. And I love remembering how each of those passages is bathed in grace.

Romans 12 begins with Paul pleading for transformed minds "by the mercies of God." In Romans 12:3, he specifically mentions "the grace given to me."

1 Corinthians 15:58 concludes the resurrection chapter. The chapter begins with grace: "the gospel I preached to you, which you received, and in which you stand." Verse 10 includes, "But by the grace of God, I am what I am…" The victory extolled in 15:57 is victory over sin and death through grace. It initiates the new life.

Ephesians 4:7 reminds us, "But grace was given to each one of us according to the measure of Christ's gift." We live up to and appreciate that grace through our consistent godly living and spiritual growth.

Philippians 2 begins with grace—our "encouragement in Christ," our "comfort from love," and our "participation in the Spirit." From that grace flows our sacrifice and selflessness.

Titus 2:11 grounds the paragraph in the fact that "the grace of God has appeared bringing salvation for all people." That grace teaches us and warns us. It both demands and empowers consistent godly living.

Titus 2:13 reminds us that through that same grace God has "purified for himself a people of his own possession who are zealous for good works." Our purification, our motivation, and our identity are grounded in grace.

1 Peter 4:7–11 reminds us that we are "to serve one another as good stewards of God's varied grace." All we have is meant for the glory of God and the good of others. That's consistent grace!

Atmosphere

No group on earth is more blessed than the Lord's church! "According to His great mercy," God Himself "has caused us to be born again to a living hope through the resurrection of Jesus Christ ..." (1 Pet 1:3). He reserves for us "an inheritance that is imperishable, undefiled, and unfading" (1 Pet 1:4).

Through the righteousness of Jesus Christ, "... His divine power has granted to us all things that pertain to life and godliness ..." (2 Pet 1:1–3). He has given us "his precious and very great promises ..." (2 Pet 1:4). He has "blessed us in Christ with every spiritual blessing in the heavenly places" (Eph 1:3).

Every time we meet, we assemble as the redeemed. We come together as the chosen. We gather as those who have been adopted by God, welcomed into His family through the gift of His Son (Eph 1:3–12).

We worship together in an atmosphere permeated by faith, hope, and love. We sing with grace in our hearts. We teach and encourage one another because the word of Christ dwells richly within us (Col 3:16). We offer and God accepts "the sacrifice of praise to God, that is, the fruit of our lips that acknowledge His name" (Heb 13:15). He accepts our worship because we have turned our hearts toward Him. As we worship and live under the authority of Jesus, God makes us ever more thankful for each opportunity to serve (Col 3:17).

Even before we come to worship, we prepare our hearts through prayer. We think fondly of one another, anticipating each opportunity "to stir up one another to love and good works" (Heb 10:24). We examine our lives so that we can commune with the Lord and with our brethren in the joy of a pure faith. We purpose in our hearts to give willingly and joyously to God (2 Cor 9:6–9).

No group on earth is more blessed than the Lord's church! When the saints meet, God meets with us. He is our joy. He is our hope. He is our life. What an atmosphere of victory and growth!

Love

A new commandment I give to you, that you love one another; just as I have loved you, you also are to love one another. By this all people will know that you are my disciples, if you have love for one another. John 13:34–35

We live in shrill, mistrusting, and accusatory times. So many seem to have chips on their shoulders, anxious for the next opportunity to fight. Examples abound:

- For some, holding a door open is seen as sexist or ageist behavior.
- For some, "Happy Holidays" is heard as an attempt to undermine Christmas.
- For others "Merry Christmas" is an attack on every other religion.
- For some, there's no blessing in public discourse or debate. It's more a matter of attacking the character and impugning the motives of all who disagree.
- For some, there's a willingness to label and discount the uniqueness of others without even giving them a chance to be heard.

And in such a world, we are still called to love. We are called to love our brethren and to trust that love to identify us as followers of Christ. We are called to love our enemies and to trust our Lord to use that love to bless both them and us (Matt 5:43–48, Rom 12:17–21). In love, we're not to provoke ill will or fuel conflict (Eph 4:29–32). Rather, we are called to kindness and encouragement as we seek to impart grace to those around us.

Clearly, we can't always tell people what they want to hear. To do so would be to forsake both truth and love. Remember Paul's example in Galatians 4:16 and the example of Jesus in Matthew 23, especially comparing the rest of the chapter with the lament in verses 37–39. Just as clearly, we must continually find ways to be "speaking the truth in love" (Eph 4:15). Nothing in Scripture implies that this will be easy, but everything in Scripture tells us that holding on to love is essential (Matt 22:34–40, 1 John 4:7–11).

So what do we do in these increasingly shrill, mistrusting, and accusatory times? We guard our hearts and our tongues. Every harmful word flows from an impure heart (Matt 12:33–37).

We weigh our words and their potential consequences. We dare not set hate in motion or fuel the fires of harm (Jas 3:5–6). Our hearts and tongues are tuned toward grace (Eph 5:29).

We look for ways to be civil and positive. Consider Acts 26. In a most negative, dangerous, and unfair setting, note how Paul maintained civility and politeness toward those who were judging him, especially addressing Agrippa as king and complimenting Festus.

We avoid the false path of peace at any price, but we embrace the wisdom of Romans 12:18. Our goal is not to win arguments; our goal is to win souls.

We love the sweet and powerful assertion: "What love cannot do, cannot be done." There is much truth in those words. He who yells longest and loudest may seem to win, but God remains the true, fair, righteous, and all-knowing judge. God will have the last word. God's love is never wrong.

Kindness

Praise the Lord, all nations! Extol him, all peoples. For great is his steadfast love toward us, and the faithfulness of the Lord endures forever. Praise the Lord! Psalm 117:2

Love is patient and kind. ... 1 Corinthians 13:4

But the fruit of the Spirit is love, joy, peace, patience, kindness. ... Galatians 5:22

And be kind to one another, tenderhearted. ... Ephesians 4:32

Kindness creates. It opens minds and hearts. Virtually every friendship begins with it. Few Bible studies succeed without it. It's a crucial part of vibrant marriages, loving families, and growing, united churches.

Kindness educates. It trains us to see people's needs and to appreciate their perspectives. It increases our awareness of opportunities to do good. It helps us find ways to open doors and show people what Jesus is like.

Kindness rejuvenates. It warms and welcomes. It enlivens and encourages. It's a day brightener and a load lifter. It removes barriers, reduces friction, and heals wounds.

Kindness reciprocates. It brings innumerable blessings to its giver. Virtually everyone is glad to encounter a kind person. A kind person is heard with more trust and respect. The mere mention of a kind person's name brings smiles and words of praise.

Kindness multiplies. It's almost infectious. As kindness touches us, we relax. We free our hearts to see the humor or at least the humanity in trying situations. Kindness helps us focus on what's right and best before God, rather than on who's right and who wins in the moment.

Kindness compels. It demands that we treat folks better than they deserve (Gen 1:26-27, Matt 5:43-48, Rom 12:17-21). It insists that we speak the whole truth in love (Eph 4:15). Real kindness won't sink into the sentimentality of "whatever you believe and however you live is okay." It can never be satisfied unless it is helping people toward heaven.

Perspective

Back in the days of the Alpha Center (a group of Christian counselors), Monnie answered the phone. The caller's question was, "Does that older gentleman still work with you?" Yep, she meant me. And that didn't bother me at all.

I knew my dad would enjoy the news of my advanced years. When I told him, he had the perfect reply: "What would she call me?"

In many respects age is just a number, and a relative number at that. When you're five, teens look old. As a teen, forty is ancient. After forty, not much looks ancient anymore.

My "advanced" age has given me new perspective on Genesis 25:7-8: "These are the days of Abraham's life, 175 years. Then Abraham breathed his last and died in a good old age, an old man, and full of years, and was gathered to his people." There's the familiar redundancy of language. The information could have been given more succinctly, but hardly more poetically or more honorably. The passage conveys major respect for a life well lived.

Abraham's 175 years make me feel a bit less like "that older gentleman." His story reminds us that there's a blessing in dying at "a good old age," but there's also a blessing in getting to see the Lord sooner. We're blessed to read Genesis 25:7-8 in conjunction with Philippians 1:19-26. People who trust God are blessed to trust Him with their very lives.

"Full of years" invites us to think: "Full in what ways?" While the primary idea may be that 175 years is a long time in human terms, Abraham lived actively and abundantly. He lived fully and faithfully. He lived a godly and generous life. We all want the same to be said of us. We're blessed to value the life in our days more than merely the number of our days.

Abraham "was gathered to his people." He didn't disappear; he went home. Death isn't presented as a void or a defeat. In prospect of Christ, the resurrection, and ultimate victory over sin, death is presented as the door to a homecoming.

We don't make light of death, as it is, in at least some senses, our enemy (1 Cor 15:26 and 54–58). We don't make light of loss or grief, as even Jesus wept with His grieving friends (John 11:35). But we take great delight in the fact that Jesus Christ has conquered death. We take great delight in the fact that His resurrection guarantees ours. We take great delight in the fact that when He returns, "the dead in Christ shall rise first" (1 Thess 4:16).

My advancing age gives me new perspective on Revelation 2:10b. "Be faithful unto death and I will give you the crown of life." We're determined to be faithful for all our days. We're determined to be faithful no matter the cost or the consequences. We're determined to "be faithful unto death" because "The one who conquers will not be hurt by the second death" (Rev 2:11). That's a God-given perspective that we can embrace with joy.

All the Difference in the World

And just as it is appointed for man to die once, and after that comes judgment, so Christ having been offered once to bear the sins of many will appear a second time, not to deal with sin, but to save those who are eagerly waiting for him. Hebrews 9:27-28

I was honored to have a part in the funeral of a good friend who was an exemplary Christian. He lived with integrity. He worked with dedication. He loved his family with all his heart. He honored God with his speech and his conduct. He made the people around him better.

As has been the case many times before, our job at the funeral was easy. Because time wouldn't allow us to share them all, we got to choose from the many happy stories and good deeds. We were able to talk about how severe illness never robbed our brother of his kindness or his sense of humor. We were able to talk of hope and heaven with confidence and conviction.

In many ways, death is one of the most unpleasant facts of life. We miss the good people who bless our lives. We hurt with our friends as they grieve. But we know that death is different for Christians.

Every good deed that they have ever done has been noticed and appreciated by the God of heaven and earth. Every prayer that they have ever prayed has risen before the throne of God as a sweet offering. Every sin that they have ever committed has been fully atoned by the blood of Jesus. And every hope that we have of sweet reunion is backed by the promise of God.

Death comes to all, but it doesn't come equally to all. "Blessed are the dead who die in the Lord from now on. 'Blessed indeed,' says the Spirit, that they may rest from their labors for their deeds follow them." (Rev 14:13). In life and in death, being in Christ makes all the difference in the world.

Advantages

Everyone to whom much was given, of him much will be required, and from him whom they entrusted much, they will demand the more. Luke 12:48

What do you have that you have not been given? More precisely, what do you have that you gained or achieved strictly on your own without assistance?

Our very being is a gift from God (Acts 17:28). He created the planet on which we stand, the air we breathe, and the sun that warms us (Gen 1). Every higher capacity and capability flows from having been created in His image (Gen 1:26–27).

From a human perspective, we're born helpless, utterly dependent on others for survival. In the formative years where one might be able to survive "on his own," both capacities and opportunities would be stunningly diminished without ongoing help from others.

On top of that, few of us would dare to claim to be self-educated. "Self-educated" is a fascinatingly ironic concept. Only with major qualification could the phrase have any hint of truth. Even if a person taught himself to read, he would do so using material written by others. And it gets even sillier if we claim to be "self-made."

What the world calls "advantages," we count as blessings. By either label, virtually all of us have more than our share. Even if some items don't apply, the following list invites thought: loving parents, access to education, meaningful work, a livable wage, access to health care, decent neighbors, precious memories, awareness of God, knowledge of His word, the fellowship of His church, the hope of heaven, the comfort of prayer, the capacity to give, the capacity to grow, and the capacity to love.

Many forget their advantages. The devil moves them to focus on what others have and what's been denied. Such deficit-centered thinking robs people of the joy of using and celebrating their gifts. It uses envy or expectation to hide God's gifts.

Others forget differently, pridefully. They persuade themselves that their gifts are their doing and their "property." They lose gratitude and the blessings that it brings.

But some remember their advantages. They thank God for the special people who have helped them learn and grow. They use their advantages to God's glory (Matt 5:13–16). And they welcome the additional blessings and opportunities that God sends (Matt 25:21–23). We are wise to be among them.

When our son Allen was in Johns Hopkins Hospital, he was blessed with many excellent nurses. Rarely did he experience a "non-excellent" caregiver. To be fair, even those few "non-excellent" people were average or above. Knowing that powerfully reminds us that compared to excellent, average looks awful.

We see hints of that in Scripture. There was much to commend "those who were scattered because of the persecution that arose over Stephen" (Acts 11:19). In the spirit of Acts 8:4, they "went about preaching the word," but they were one step short of excellent. Acts 11:19 tells us that they were "speaking the word to no one except Jews." They had not yet caught the truth that the gospel is to be preached to "all nations" (Matt 28:19) and "to the whole creation"

(Mark 16:15).

Some Christians knew better. Some did more. Some excelled in evangelism. They "spoke to the Hellenists also, preaching the Lord Jesus" (Acts 11:20). The next verse is beautiful: "And the hand of the Lord was with them, and a great number believed and turned to the Lord." It's good to evangelize, but it's even better to evangelize boldly to all who will hear without regard to status or ethnicity.

There was much to commend the Thessalonian Christians. Paul rightly praised their "work of faith and labor of love, and steadfastness of hope" (1 Thess 1:3). He rightly praised them as "an example to all the believers in Macedonia and Achaia" (1 Thess 1:7). But as a whole, the people in Thessalonica paled in comparison to the Bereans. Acts 17:11 says, "Now these Jews were more noble than those in Thessalonica; they received the word with all eagerness, examining the Scriptures daily to find out whether these things were so." Fair-mindedness, readiness, and respect for Scripture speak of excellence.

The same point is made in the parable of the virgins (Matt 25:1–13). All "took their lamps and went to meet the bridegroom." All napped when the bridegroom was delayed; and nothing negative is said of that. The difference was that five went the second mile in preparation; they took extra oil. Five did not. Five excelled. The average five failed.

We see the same point in the healing of the ten lepers (Luke 17:11–19). Ten were healed. All ten obediently started to see the priests. Only one returned to glorify God and give thanks. His faith and gratitude were praised by Jesus. And without any bad motive or action, his righteous excellence made the thoughtless nine look awful.

Every Christian is called to abound in the work of the Lord

(1 Cor 15:58) and in godly virtue (2 Pet 1:8). The Lord deserves our constant best and more (1 Thess 4:9–11).

People Are Something

He who justifies the wicked and he who condemns the righteous are both alike an abomination to the Lord.
Proverbs 17:15

Think of the biblical examples of those who condemned the just. As Moses worked for their deliverance, the officers of the children of Israel railed on Moses for making them "stink in the sight of Pharaoh and his servants" (Exod 5:21). Just before the great miracle of deliverance at the Red Sea, the people insultingly asked Moses, "Is it because there were no graves in Egypt, have you taken us away to die in the wilderness?" (Exod 14:11). It's as if they had amnesia about requesting God's help in securing their freedom (Exod 14:12). In Exodus 16:2-3, the whole congregation complained, "Would that we had died by the hand of the Lord in the land of Egypt. … For you have brought us out into this wilderness to kill the whole assembly with hunger." They impugned Moses' motive and judged his character. Really, they were questioning the goodness and honesty of God.

It's bad enough when enemies practice such foolishness. It's worse when your own people attack you. How bad must it be when your own family joins in? Remember the sad account of Numbers 12. Though Moses was "very meek, more than all people who were on the face of the earth," Aaron and Miriam accused him of taking too strong a leadership role (Num 12:1-3). At least they accused him of failing to appreciate their roles in leadership. Had Moses not interceded, God would have slain them both for condemning the just. At least this sad episode prepared Moses for the events of Numbers 16—the accusations of self-exaltation leveled by Korah.

Jesus spoke of this to His disciples as recorded in John 16:2, "They will put you out of the synagogues. Indeed the hour is coming that whoever kills you will think he is offering service to God." How could people be so wrong?

Think of the biblical examples of those who justified the wicked. Think of Aaron's attempt to justify himself in the matter of the golden calf (Exod 32:22-25). Though aged Eli spoke against the wickedness of his sons, he did not restrain them—something that was within his power to do (1 Sam 2). The Lord viewed this as kicking at His sacrifice and honoring his sons ahead of God. Remember the lawyer who wanted "to justify himself" as he asked Jesus, "And who is my neighbor?" (Luke 10:25-37) Think of the "justification" offered by Caiaphas in John 11:50, "… it is better for you that one man should die for the people, not that the whole nation should perish."

As we contemplate these examples, we draw several important implications:

- No person can be so good that his motives or actions will never be questioned.
- No action can be so good or pure that some won't question or criticize it.
- No person can be so evil that some won't defend his actions and motives.
- We need God's wisdom to "judge with righteous judgment"

(John 7:24) and to "walk in wisdom" (Col 4:5). We're tremendously blessed that ultimate judgment belongs to God who always gets it right.

It's Easier to Do Right

It's easier to do right than to wish that you had. Do you hear that statement as proverb, truism, or cliché? I lean toward truism, but the reason for that is elusive.

"It's easier to do right than" makes a thought-provoking sentence starter. Consider these options and feel free to add your own.

It's easier to do right than to deal with the consequences of a less noble choice. Think of lying King Saul in 1 Samuel 15 and the Amalekite in 2 Samuel 1.

It's easier to do right than to face the guilt of letting God down. Think of David in Psalm 51 and Judas in Matthew 27.

It's easier to do right than to try to explain why you didn't. Think of Adam and Eve in Genesis 3 and Aaron in Exodus 32.

It's easier to do right than to let yourself down. Think of Paul in Romans 7.

Maybe we should change the sentence starter and think further.

It's better to do right than to miss the blessings that the right action will bring. Think of the conflict between Abram and Lot in Genesis 13.

It's better to do right than to let evil erode your character. Think of Cain in Genesis 4.

It's better to do right than to give in to the status quo. Think

Romans 12:1–2.

It's better to do right than to let your critics be right. Think of David and his brother in 1 Samuel 17:28-29.

It's better to do right than to give the devil a foothold. Think of Ephesians 4:27.

It's better to do right than to put your family in harm's way. Think of Achan in Joshua 7.

It's better to do right and rely on God to settle accounts. Think of Colossians 3:23–24.

It's better to do right even if that puts your life in danger. Think of Daniel's three friends in Daniel 3 and Daniel himself in Daniel 6.

It's better to do right, even it costs you your life. Think of Revelation 2:10, Hebrews 11:35–40, and John in Matthew 14. Bluntly, it's just always better to do right for the right reason to God's glory, no matter what the immediate outcome.

Life Can Slow You Down

Life can slow you down. Life can stop you in your tracks. Life can suspend your engagements, change your calendar, and make your plans obsolete. And it can do this in a moment (Luke 12:16–21).

Life can break your heart. It can teach you more about tears and trouble than you ever wanted to learn (Job 1–2). In the same situations, it can teach you so much about grace and gratitude. In every crisis come unexpected strengths, resources, and opportunities. The challenge is to see those assets through the fog of our feelings.

Life can wear you out. There's the good tired of working hard and seeing progress. The tired that comes from watching and waiting doesn't feel like that. Emotional fatigue is different. It's partly being out of your element and off your schedule. But it's much more a matter of realizing human limitations. We need God's help to keep going (Gal 6:9).

Life can make you wonder. What if I'd done this or said that? Would life be notably, positively different? This isn't the wise wondering of godly self-examination. It's the devilish game of replaying the past in light of the present, wondering why you didn't know what you couldn't have known. It's the wondering that punishes and paralyzes without benefit.

Life can shut you up. It can push you to withdraw from the

relationships that bless you the most. Misery doesn't always love company. For good folks, misery often seeks solitude. You don't feel like being with anyone. You don't want to be a burden to anyone. You absolutely don't want to be around people who try to tell you how you should feel. And if you're not really careful in times of major pain, you'll wrongly put everyone into that group.

Life can hem you in. It can keep you out of places that bless your heart and soul. You can forget the power of a sunset, a rainbow, a park, or a garden. You can even, for a time, forget the power of the happiest of memories. The devil being what he is, he will even try to use the challenges of life to make you feel like you aren't entitled to your own best memories. It's as if he says, "If you enjoy anything, past or present, you aren't taking life seriously today." It's classic double-bind. You feel bad for even trying to feel good.

Life can make you want to quit. Does anything we do really make a difference? Can any human make this world a better place? Jesus did. Jesus does. His people do by His grace and through His power. We don't win every battle, but He gives us victory (Rom 8).

Life can mess with your head. Life can mess with your health. Life can mess with your heart. It's much too fragile, important, powerful, and complicated to leave to human wisdom. This time the bumper sticker has it right: "LIFE: HANDLE WITH PRAYER."

Fragile

As for man, his days are like grass; he flourishes like as a flower of the field, so he flourishes, for the wind passes over it, and it is gone, and its place knows it no more.
Psalm 103:15–16

In many ways, humans are stunningly tough. God has blessed us with physiological redundancies. Our vital organs are strategically placed and well-shielded. When injury occurs, even the brain shows remarkable ability to heal.

On the other hand, we're also stunningly fragile. We can be killed by organisms that are invisible to us. We can be plagued by diseases that will prove fatal but currently show no symptoms. From a stray bullet to a wreck, life can end in an instant. And though the wind in Psalm 103 doesn't speak of a tornado, we can't read the verse without thinking of the most recent deadly storm.

Bottom line: from the perspective of human mortality, we're as fragile as the flower of the field. But, we're fragile in other ways as well. The best-built home can't stand the direct hit of a tornado. Electric lines fall with the impact of a single tree. Without electricity, we can't get gasoline from the station. If the media mentions that fact, panic buying ensues, and there's no gas to get. And without electricity and gasoline, our emotional fragility becomes evident.

What's a Christian to do in light of these truths about our fragile nature? Proverbs 3:5–6 comes to mind: "Trust in the Lord with all your heart, and do not lean on your own understanding. In all your ways acknowledge him, and he will make straight your paths." There are dangers that can't be avoided. There are problems that can't be solved in this world. But walking with God is walking toward a better world. Walking with God is never being alone or forsaken (Heb 13:5). Walking with God is keeping our spiritual hope grounded on The Rock.

There are many things we can't fathom. How folks face fragility without God is near the top of that list. I could not; I dare not. God is too good and this world is too dangerous to run such risk or to face such uncertainty.

How We Need to Pray!

And he told them a parable to the effect that they ought always to pray and not lose heart. Luke 18:1

Life can be stunningly difficult. Countless situations exceed our limited understanding. When the challenges of life again overwhelm our capacity to cope, how we need to pray! Without God's help, we are sure to lose heart.

A good family waits for a palliative care room to become available. They need the room for a loved one, but they know what it takes for that room to become available. It's the same as the family awaiting a room in the nursing home. They need relief from the demands of constant care, but they don't want that relief to come at cost to others. How we need to pray!

Families are laying children to rest, children who perished in the latest school shooting. It didn't have to be, it served no purpose, and it blessed no one. Nonetheless, their world is changed forever. Precious dreams are gone. How we need to pray!

A fine young man's world has just come apart. His wife has left him. In one sense, it doesn't matter why. There is no sufficient reason to break covenant with God and the one to whom you've pledged your heart. Things won't ever be the same. How we need to pray!

Elders want to spare feelings and limit the damage of an

unwinnable situation. Perhaps it would be better to tell less than the truth. Perhaps a little untruth might help this hurting church. But nothing good ever came of a lie. Truth, honor, and integrity dare not be sacrificed on the altar of feelings. How we need to pray!

A preacher nears his breaking point. He has borne all the disappointment that his heart can bear. Career change begins to seem essential. And if he changes careers, there's less harm in burning the bridges that he's about to burn. In the moment, he can't seem to remember that there are precious people standing on those bridges. How we need to pray!

A struggling Christian uses all remaining strength to drag herself to worship, hoping for a blessing from God and His people. Instead of a warm greeting, she is told, "I wish you wouldn't come in late. I find that very distracting." And her parting thought is, "I will never distract you again." How we need to pray!

Every day isn't sunny—even if the sun is bright. Every day isn't easy. Many don't have the support and blessings that we do. Some don't even know that God offers those blessings. We are sometimes know of struggles in others' lives, but often we don't have a clue. How we need to pray—for family, friends, enemies, strangers, and for ourselves.

> *Lord, open our eyes to see, and open our hearts to care. Lord, help us turn our good intentions into acts of loving service. Lord, help us to guard our thoughts and our words. Lord, help us to know how we need to pray, and help us to pray as if our souls depend on You. Lord, help us to pray in the name, in the will, and in the heart of Jesus. Lord, help us to act to make our prayers as real to us as they are to You. In the precious name of Jesus, amen.*

Weather Woes

Through the winter, we lamented the snow and ice. We couldn't wait for the weather to warm. Some of us even promised, "I'll never complain about the heat again!"

Then, we had rain, rain, and more rain. We couldn't wait for sunny dry days. But during the summer, we'd love to see it rain on our parched lawns.

When, the record heat is the talk of the town, We wonder, "How will we pay our utility bills?" "Is it hot enough for you?"

And none of this holds a candle to the tragedies caused by floods and tornadoes to towns and cities near us. Most of us are merely inconvenienced by our weather woes.

What's a Christian to do? How do we keep our spirits up and our attitudes right? How do we avoid the descent into grumbling and whining?

- We can choose praying over grumbling (Phil 4:6).
- We can choose trust and thanksgiving over worry and fear (Phil 4:6–7).
- We can choose following godly examples over following the path of least resistance (Phil 4:9).
- We can choose meditating on the true, honorable, just, pure, lovely, and commendable over emphasizing our pains, losses, fears, defeats, aggravations, and disappointments

(Phil 4:8).
- We can choose helping others over seeking to be helped by others (Phil 4:10–12).
- We can choose trusting the promises of God over trusting our own sight and reasoning (Phil 4:6–7 and 9).
- We can choose celebrating our blessings over focusing on our trials (Phil 4:4–5).
- We can choose contentment over complaining. Paul did so under far more challenging conditions than those faced by most of us (Phil 4:10–13).

Are these easy choices? Hardly. They demand faith, vision, knowledge, and maturity. They demand an upward focus that's contrary to the ways of this world (Col 3:1–5, 2 Cor 5:7). They demand valuing the spiritual above the material, valuing the eternal above the temporal. They demand self-discipline and "swimming against the current" of the world. While these choices are anything but easy, they are the path to peace, joy, and contentment. They are the path to good living now and forevermore.

On Storms and Attitudes

... For I have learned in whatever situation I am to be content. Philippians 4:11

Therefore do not be anxious about tomorrow, for tomorrow will be anxious for itself. Sufficient for the day is its own trouble. Matthew 6:34

People's attitudes toward bad weather amaze me. A friend recently told me that he sat up watching the weather on TV so that he wouldn't blow away. It never occurred to me that watching weather on TV could prevent the impact of a storm. I know he was using shorthand to say that he was being diligent and "weather aware," but the way he said it struck me oddly. Aware and safe are related, but separate, ideas.

In childhood, our plan for bad weather was to go to bed at bedtime. If the wind blew the sheet off the bed or rain hit us in the face, then we'd adjust accordingly. If not, we'd wait for daylight and start doing what needed to be done. And I know that's not the best plan.

I'm not a storm chaser. I have no desire to maximize the risk. At the same time, storms—neither predicted nor actual—cause me much anxiety. Part of that may be due to personality—though not unflappable, I don't think I'm easily "flapped." Part of that has to do with the blessing of good parents. Through the years they have suffered numerous losses due to storms, but they never lost their faith or optimism. They aren't given to worry or panic. Part of that has to do with confidence in prayer. There's mystery in how God protects His own, but we know that He does. Even when He doesn't spare property and lives, He never loses a soul that loves Him (Rom 8:31–39).

Twice, way back when, we lost electricity during storms. Each time, two of the neighbor's trees fell across the power lines. An old TV and a few other items "cooked," but the losses were light. Each storm reminded us of how dependent we are on electricity. Each reminded us of how stunningly convenient our lives are most days. Each reminded us to thank God for the good and easy days and for the ability to endure the storms. Each reminded us that most challenging storms aren't weather-related, and that we sure need to help one another when those storms come (2 Cor 11:28–29).

Sweet Words

Sweet words lift our spirits and strengthen our souls. We love to hear them because they feel good as they bless us. We gravitate toward people who speak sweet words. I hope we also imitate those people and their words. Just as destructive words carry tremendous power for evil, sweet words—truthful, loving, gracious words—carry tremendous power for good.

What a joy to catch somebody using sweet words to promote unity and harmony. What a blessing to enhance the joy by remembering to say, "Thank you for being a peacemaker. Jesus pronounced a blessing on people like you (Matt 5:9). Solomon wrote about people like you (Prov 15:1). So did Paul (Eph 4:29). I'm glad I know you. You encourage me."

What a joy to catch somebody using sweet words to promote faithfulness and spiritual growth. What a blessing to enhance that joy by remembering to say, "Thank you for reminding me of the truth of Philippians 2:1–4 and Hebrews 10:24. I've noticed how you consistently look for ways to help others through your words. I want you to know how much I appreciate the way you bless others."

What a joy to catch somebody using sweet words to teach a child or a fellow struggler. I know that none of us teach perfectly, but sometimes God blesses us with the right words at the right time and we experience the joy of Proverbs 25:11. What a blessing to enhance that joy by remembering to say, "My, that was well done. I see the spirit of Christ in your words (Acts 4:13). You make the people around you better. I thought of 1 Peter 4:7–11 when I heard you teaching."

What a joy to catch somebody using sweet words, gently and wisely, to warn and challenge a brother who is in spiritual danger. What a blessing to enhance that joy by remembering to say, "Thank you for your courage. I know it would have been easier to keep silent (Gal 2:11–21, 4:16). Thank you for knowing that loving words of warning are sweet to God's ears. Thank you for your wisdom and balance (Prov 26:4–5). Thank you for listening before you spoke (Prov 18:13 and 29:20). Thank you for saying enough without saying too much (Prov 10:19–21 and 29:11). Thank you for inviting our brother to consider God's wisdom and to invite God's help."

What a joy to catch ourselves using sweet words to the glory of God. What a blessing to enhance that joy by remembering to say,

> *Lord, thank you for the continual guidance of Your word (Ps 19:7–11). Thank you for the example of Your Son. Lord, help me watch my words and to use every one of them to Your glory (Ps 19:14, Prov 31:26). In Jesus name amen*

Sweet words come in many forms, but some seem particularly obvious.

- Expressions of appreciation: "Thank you." "I appreciate that." "I appreciate you."
- Both offers of and requests for help: "Can I help you?" "I need your help." "Can you help me, please?"
- Expressions of love and connection: "I love you." "I value our friendship." "I'm glad I know you."

- Words of repentance and restoration: "I was wrong." "I'm sorry." "Please forgive me."

It's amazing how easily these words come to some and how difficult they are for others. We know there are many reasons for this. We learn so much from our respective families of origin. Those of us who were blessed with excellent models as children have tremendous advantage. Those who were shown a bad pattern but chose God's better way merit special commendation. It's such a challenge to live better than we were reared.

Some are born with sweeter, more thoughtful dispositions than others. I used to think that every child was born with a "blank slate" and became what parents taught them to become. While never denigrating the power of godly parenting, I'm now certain that aspects of personality have strong genetic links. I'm just as sure that a measure of sweetness can be learned. If one of the "sons of thunder" could become the "apostle of love", each of us can grow with God's help.

Some pay too much attention to gender stereotypes and cultural expectations. One of the devil's most effective lies is that real men don't say, "I love you." Another is—"to quote the famous movie line," "Never apologize. It's a sign of weakness." But we know that righting a wrong is really a spiritual strength (Matt 5:23–24). Saying "I love you" is powerful every time that it's true (John 13:34–35). At least to some degree, our words have performative power. We want to live up to our words. Saying the right things can move us one step closer to doing the right things.

Some suffer having their sweet, heartfelt words rejected. None of us like to feel "bit." We remember the pain, and logic tells us to avoid the pain by stopping the behavior that caused it. How we need to be careful! Sweet, honest, heartfelt words don't cause rejection. The rejection comes from inside the rejecter (Gal 4:16, 2 Cor 7:2–12). We cannot control how others respond to us or our words.

Some have not practiced sweet words enough to feel comfortable with them. Practice tends to improve our comfort level, but getting started can be a major challenge. For some, the key is to practice before speaking. For others, a key might be putting sweet words into print—sweet cards, notes, letters, texts, and tweets—before verbalizing them. The real key is getting unstuck and finding the courage to move from good intentions to good actions.

One suggestion for starting: If you have thought something sweet but have not yet said it, find a way. Break the ice. Take the risk. Use the energy from your success to win the next victory. Sweet words come from sweet hearts. Sweet words often sweeten our hearts. And God loves sweet, faithful, loving hearts.

Saying What We Mean and Meaning What We Say

> ... *For we all stumble in many ways, and if anyone does not stumble in what he says, he is a perfect man, able also to bridle his whole body. James 3:2*

Truer words have never been written! It's hard to get our words right. I once received a description of an upcoming meal. It included the line, "I'll be cooking lasagna and salad." I know what she meant, but I'd rather have my salad uncooked.

A repairman made a stop at our house. After looking me over he asked, "Didn't you used to be a preacher?" While some might disagree, I told him that I was still trying.

A friend reminisced about one of his grandmother's favorite sayings: "I feel tough today." Most of us know what she meant. She wasn't claiming to feel strong or sturdy. She wasn't claiming to feel durable or indestructible. She was merely telling the world that she wasn't feeling well.

Laura once wrote an article about procrastination. She included a line about being a faithful steward of time. In the first version of the article, she had a line that included the words "steward (stewardess?)." She wanted an opinion as to which word to use. Technically, "stewardess" is both correct and gender-specific. But I recommended "steward," and I think you know why. For most of us age forty and older, "stewardess" enters the mind as "flight attendant." Airline employees had nothing to do with Laura's point.

All this makes me want to be increasingly careful with my words. James 3 strongly supports that. A few wrong words can be as dangerous as a match in the driest forest (Jas 3:5–6). A few wrong words can unleash beasts of emotion that cannot be tamed.

But all this also makes me want to be increasingly kind in how I hear the words of others. My friend Cory Collins sometimes talks about "behavioral ambiguity." Certain behaviors are highly open to interpretation. When that's the case, choose the kindest and most gracious view. There's also "verbal ambiguity." When that's the case, we can follow the very same rule.

For example, "It's good to see you, **old** friend," can offend. "Why are you calling me old? In comparison to what am I old? I don't feel old. Why are you insulting me? Alternately, "Yes, I'm old, but why are you reminding me?"

The same words can be heard so positively. "It's good to see you, old **friend**." I love it when someone affirms our friendship. It's so pleasant to think of the miles that we've traveled together, the victories we've shared, and the challenges that God has helped us endure. You are one of the best treasures that God has placed in my life!

The same words heard by unique individuals in their varied moods and circumstances often get very different hearings. May God help us to speak and hear better (Prov 17:27–28, 25:11–12, 26:18–22, 27:2, 29:11, and 31:26; Jas 1:19–20)!

Giving and Keeping Our Word

David begins Psalm 15 with two great questions. "O Lord, who shall sojourn in your tent? Who shall dwell in Your holy hill?"

Among the many great answers are these words from Psalm 15:4, "He who swears to his own hurt and does not change." You know what David means. The person "who walks blamelessly, and does what is right, and speaks truth in his heart" is the person who gives and keeps his word (Ps 15:2).

I like the entertainment of college football. It's unpredictable and fun. Stars sometimes shine, but sometimes fail. Unknowns rise to the occasion and become stars. Experts often get to eat their words. And if my team didn't do great, there's always next year.

I hate some of the ways that college football reflects the very worst of our culture. Young men are tempted to pride and self-destruction because they can outrun, out-catch, and out-hit others. Some fans live down to the word "fanatic," almost worshiping the sport and its stars. Thousands gamble on the sport. Many give it more attention than they give to their own souls and the souls of their neighbors.

One of the most negative aspects of college football directly intersects Psalm 15:4. Coaches give their word to schools and players. It's some version of "You can trust me. I'm here to stay. We're going to build a great program together. I'm not going anywhere." But as soon as more money or a bigger stage is offered, they're gone.

Some of the "explanations" blow me away, particularly the often used line, "I had to do what was best for my family." How could it be best for one's family to lie? How could it be best for anyone to value money and convenience over honor, character, and veracity?

We live in cynical times. Most people don't value their own word. Cynicism is reinforced every time a public figure belies himself. The unstated messages are clear. Who can you trust? Why trust anyone? After all, every person has his price. It's all just a game.

In light of such thinking, some around us have adopted a "no expectations" approach to truth and honesty. They never expect others to tell the truth and to keep their word. That way, they're never disappointed. What a discouraging approach to life!

Jesus had it right. He understood the simplicity and blessing of basic honesty. He understood the danger of playing "fast and loose" with our word. "Let what you say be simply 'Yes' or 'No;' anything more than this comes from evil" (Matt 5:37). Jesus stingingly forbids "verbal gamesmanship" in Matthew 23. As the way, the truth, and the life, Jesus knew, emphasized, and embodied the value of truth. He calls us to do the same. What an opportunity for us to be better and different in Christ!

The Destructive Power of Bad Words

Is there anything that bad words can't harm? Think of the latest example of racist language. Even if the speaker apologizes profusely, damage has been done. Everyone knows the evil words never should have been thought or spoken. Regrettably, some will defend or excuse the slurs. Others will withhold forgiveness even when apologies seem sincere.

Thanks be to God that we can be better than the world around us. While we know we are influenced by culture, we can rise above it. Noah proves that from Genesis 6:5-8. So do Joseph, Daniel, and Jesus.

When it comes to slurs, insults, lies, and the like, several passages can guide and protect us:

- Proverbs 29:11, "A fool gives full vent to his spirit, but a wise man quietly holds it back."
- Proverbs 29:20, "Do you see a man hasty in his words? There is more hope for a fool than for him."
- Matthew 12:34 and 36, "For out of the abundance of the heart the mouth speaks. ... I tell you, on the day of judgment people will give account for every careless word they speak, for by your words you will be justified, and by your words you will be condemned."
- Ephesians 4:29, "Let no corrupting talk come out of your

mouths, but only such as is good for building up, as fits the occasion, that it may give grace to those who hear."
- Ephesians 4:31, "Let all bitterness and wrath and anger and clamor and slander be put away from you, along with all malice."
- Ephesians 5:4, "Let there be no filthiness, nor foolish talk, nor crude joking, which are out of place, but instead let there be giving."
- Colossians 4:6, "Let your speech always be gracious, seasoned with salt, so that you may know how you ought to answer each person."
- James 3:2 and 8, "For we all stumble in many ways. If anyone does not stumble in what he says, he is a perfect man, able also to bridle his whole body. … But human being can tame the tongue. It is a restless evil, full of deadly poison."

What applications should we draw from these passages? What we say comes from inside us, and we're responsible for it. There's no use making excuses. When we mess up, we must 'fess up.

The key to a pure and wise tongue is a pure and wise heart. Only God can give us such a heart. But we can work with God and one another to improve.

Evil words not only endanger our souls at the judgment, sometimes they have heavy immediate costs right here on earth. They harm everything from influence to relationships to earnings.

Once words escape our lips, there's no taking them back. Christians admire and appreciate genuine repentance, but many in the world do not. The world excels in holding grudges, escalating conflict, and exacting revenge.

When it comes to sound and wholesome speech, we need to hold ourselves to the very highest standard. God does. Even the people of the world expect Christians to live up to 1 Corinthians 13:4–8. We dare not expect less of ourselves.

Lying Liars and Their Lying Lies

You shall not steal. You shall not bear false witness against your neighbor. You shall not covet ... Exodus 20:15–17a

Therefore, having put away falsehood, let each one of you speak the truth with his neighbor, for we are members one of another. ... Let the thief no longer steal, but rather let him labor, doing honest work with his own hands, so that he may have something to share with anyone in need. Ephesians 4:25 and 28

... And all liars, their portion will be in the lake that burns with fire and sulfur, which is the second death. Revelation 21:8b

More than a decade ago, it came to Laura's email on October 21st—my birthday. At first glance it sounded so believable. It was a touching appeal for funds from a friend who had lost her purse and was stranded in London. She needed $2,800 wired to Western Union so that she could pay the hotel bill and be allowed to leave the country. The email ended with a verse of Scripture. Just above the Scripture was a reminder of our friend's role in her local church.

This scam was advanced for its day. The lying email was written in conversational English with few mistakes. It appealed to the basic goodness in all who would want to help a friend. In some ways, it appeared to have aspects of "truthiness."

But, we easily recognized it as a hoax. No one would need to wire cash to pay a hotel bill in London. Faxing or calling in a credit card number could handle that. Our friend has many friends. She would never need to send a mass appeal for financial help to cover $2,800. A telephone call quickly confirmed the hoax. We learned of our friend's immediate efforts to have the lying email removed from circulation.

Scams will continue to grow more sophisticated. Even back in the days of Allen's illness, we realized that the same could happen to us. Some thief could have sent an emergency appeal for funds with an address or an account number. Without proper thought or investigation, well-meaning people might have been duped into responding. And the thieves would laugh at their good fortune.

How can we defend against lying liars and their lying lies? We can choose to think. Does what I'm reading make sense? Is it internally consistent? Does it fit with common sense and reality? We can seek the opinions of trusted others. They will be blessed by helping us.

We can investigate. Nobody with a legitimate need will object to fielding pertinent questions. We can value sound action over quick action. Anything or anyone who pressures us for immediate response should be investigated. Thoughtful deliberation is not evidence of apathy or unwillingness. Rather, it's evidence of sound stewardship and good judgment. In many senses, "…the sons of this world are more shrewd in dealing with their generation than the sons of light" (Luke 16:8b). There's no virtue in being fooled!

Wisdom thinks before it acts!

Words Have Always Been Dangerous

Words are dangerous when they take the form of temptation. In Genesis 3, the serpent used subtle, negative, accusing words to tempt Eve. The words of Mrs. Potiphar in Genesis 39 are a shocking example of overt temptation. Proverbs 1:10–11 describe how some sinners entice through words. Of course, the Devil misused words, even words from Scripture, in his temptation of Christ as recorded in Matthew 4.

Words are also dangerous in the form of lies. In Genesis 3, the serpent lied when he impugned God's motives. He continued the lie in the promises that he made to Eve. Abraham's lies in Genesis 12 and 20 endangered Pharaoh and Abimelech, respectively. Jacob's lies in Genesis 27 almost cost him his life. Laban's lie in Genesis 29 began years of family pain. Lies can cost a person even more than his life (Rev 21:8).

Words are terribly dangerous in the form of false teaching. Deuteronomy 13:1–5 tells us just how serious false teaching is to God. Jesus strongly warned against false prophets in Matthew 7:15 and Matthew 24:23–24. Paul's powerful warning in Galatians 1:8–9 is unforgettable. Scripture is clear. False teachers exist in every generation. False teaching can cost people their souls!

Words can be very dangerous in the form of discouragement. We remember the enemies of Nehemiah (Neh 4:1–3). What are these feeble Jews doing? Will they complete this wall in a day? Will they revive stones from the heaps of rubbish? Even if a fox jumps on it, he will break down their stone wall. While both false teaching and false living must be opposed, we are blessed to live under the encouraging mandate of Ephesians 4:29 and Hebrews 10:24–25. We delight in encouraging one another.

Words are dangerous in the form of unspoken truth. We have responsibility to speak both the good words and the warnings that should be spoken. Remember Ezekiel 33:1–9. Remember Acts 20:26. Remember John 6:63. Jesus' words are, and ever will be, both spirit and life!

A Rare Opportunity

For we hear that some among you walk in idleness, not busy at work, but busybodies. Now such persons we command and encourage in our Lord Jesus Christ to do all their work quietly and earn their own living.
2 Thessalonians 3:11–12

Besides that, they learn to be idlers, going about from house to house and not only idlers, but also gossips and busybodies, saying what they should not.
1 Timothy 5:13

But let none of you suffer as a murderer or a thief or an evildoer or as a meddler. 1 Peter 4:15

A friend gave me a rare opportunity to consider an important question. She asked, "What do you do when people around you break into gossip?" My friend didn't want to be rude or to seem self-righteous. At the same time, she didn't want to condone evildoing by failing to act. Even more, she didn't want to be tempted to join in a commonly accepted sinful behavior (Eph 4:29–31). I appreciate her heart and her question.

Biblically speaking, one protection against gossip is to stay busy.

We know the proverb: "The one rowing the boat isn't the one rocking it." Most of us have all the business we can care for. If we're gossiping, we may be neglecting some important work. Of course, it's possible to break into gossip even while busy in good work. The devil is good at his job.

This doesn't exactly fit the case of my friend. She's not neglecting her duties. She's not initiating gossip. She's trying to protect herself from the poor judgment of others. More than that, she's looking for a way to help them escape the sin of gossip.

Perhaps, that's another key. Could she say, "I'm afraid that what I'm hearing is gossip. Is this really something that we should be discussing?" Sometimes education helps. Sometimes, ignorance is the door into temptation. Perhaps people just need a friendly reminder.

I know of a preacher who was said to keep a notebook on his desk. Whenever anyone said anything that approached gossip, he'd open the book and say, "Wait a minute. I need to get all this down accurately. When we go to talk to this brother just like Matthew 18:15–20 and Galatians 6:1–2 tell us, I want to be sure to quote you correctly." I admire his courage.

Maybe another key would be to practice the golden rule (Matt 7:12). Might it lead us to say, "You know, it discourages me when I hear that others have talked about me. I've made a commitment to practice the golden rule. I just can't let us do something to another person that I wouldn't want done to me"? Some things should not be said—even if true.

What ideas do you have for combating the sin of gossip? I'm happy to keep learning. Many others are as well.

Combating Gossip

One key to combating gossip is to realize its harm. We've heard it said, "Sticks and stones can break my bones, but words will never hurt me." That's a stunningly false statement. Words can destroy, discourage, and demoralize. Words can meddle and manipulate. Words can break friendships (Prov 16:27–30 and 18:6-8, 19 and 21). Bad words can break hearts. Bad words can damage faith and push people away from God.

The Proverbs offers strong warnings: "… A whisperer separates close friends" (Prov 16:28). "… But he who repeats a matter separates close friends" (Prov 17:9). Division is the devil's work.

Proverbs 26:18–22 also speaks to this truth. The meddler is compared to one "who throws firebrands, arrows, and death." He's the one who keeps the fire of strife going. He delivers "tasty trifles" that appeal to the baser instincts. He leads people away from God.

Another key to combating gossip is to remember how gossip makes the gossiper look. Bad words makes the gossiper look mean and malicious. They make the speaker look cold and uncaring. They make him look trite and thoughtless. They make him look injurious and judgmental. They make the gossiper look unloving and undisciplined (Eph 4:29, Prov 25:28).

Remembering judgment is another key to combating gossip. The Lord said, "I tell you, on the day of judgment, people will give account for every careless word they speak, or by your words you will be justified, and by your words you will be condemned" (Matt 12:36–37). Our words reveal our hearts. "The evil person out of his evil treasure brings forth evil" (Matt 12:35b). Evil is as evil does. Gossip is evil.

On the positive side, the consistent use of godly speech combats gossip. Ephesians 4:29 reads, "Let no corrupting talk come out of your mouths, but only such as is good for building up, as fits the occasion, that it may give grace to those who hear." Gossip is corrupt communication. Gossip never imparts grace. Even if gossip is factual, it's wrong.

Grace-imparting communication is different. Even if it's a word of warning or correction, it will be spoken to the person who needs to hear it in the right setting with an attitude of love (Matt 18:15, Gal 6:1–2). Grace-imparting communication will be spoken in the Lord's name to the Lord's glory.

On the positive side, gossip is prevented when we remember the truth of Ephesians 4:25: "… For we are members one of another." The same truth is taught in Ephesians 5:29–30, "For no one ever hated his own flesh, but nourishes and cherishes it, just as the Lord does the church. For we are members of His body, of His flesh and of His bones." We can't attack any brother or sister without hurting ourselves and our Lord.

Trouble I

… In the world you will have tribulation. … John 16:33

Scholars use the following synonyms for tribulation: affliction, difficulties, distress, frustration, oppression, persecution, sorrows, suffering, and trouble. We know that Jesus was both correct and courageous when He spoke these words. He was about to face betrayal, false accusation, mockery, torture, and death. And that's not all that Isaiah meant when he described the Messiah as "…despised and rejected by men, a man of sorrows and acquainted with grief" (Isa 53:3). Read the rest of Isaiah 53 and note the pain words: anguish, despised, oppressed, rejected, sorrow, smitten, and stricken. What stunningly sobering and accurate words!

Isn't it just like the Lord to tell people the whole truth even in the darkest hour? No hedging. No ifs. No maybes. "In the world you will have tribulation. …"

Given the Lord's clarity, why are we still so often surprised by trouble? "How could this happen to a nice person like me?" "This makes no sense." "This isn't fair." "This should not be happening." "This cannot be happening." But trouble comes to all.

I strongly believe that the Lord chose and measured His words more carefully than anyone else in history. Why was He so blunt about the inevitability of trouble? Part of the answer flows from His identity. Jesus remains "the way and the truth and the life" (John

14:6). He is always honest with us. What's true is true, even when it's neither pleasant nor desirable.

Jesus was clear about the inevitability of trouble because forewarned is forearmed. There is no need to give the devil the element of surprise. Additionally, being informed gives us opportunity to prepare on multiple levels. The following questions may help.

Are we better off facing life's troubles with God or without Him? John 16:33 ends with an amazing promise. Are we better protected as part of His loving family or on our own? Think of Philippians 2:3-4.

Are we willing to learn from life's troubles? Are we willing to ask God to guide our learning? Think deeply on Hebrews 2:9-18, 5:5-11, and 12:1-11.

Are we wiser to rail against the trouble or to look for ways to endure and overcome? We cannot change reality, no matter how many people think otherwise.

Are we willing to admit and turn from any part we played in causing some of the troubles that we face? Think of the heartfelt confessions found in Deuteronomy 32 and Daniel 9:3-19.

Are we willing to accept the blessings that God can bring through troubles? Pain can be an awesome teacher—and I do not say that lightly. Think of Psalm 119:71. Think of what affliction taught Joseph and Daniel.

Are we willing to look beyond our own troubles to the needs of others? How might our troubles make us more dependent on God, less judgmental, more understanding, and more willing to reach out to fellow strugglers? Think of 1 Thessalonians 5:14 and 20-23.

Trouble will come. It may reach the level of tribulation. When it does, will we keep trusting God and welcoming His aid?

Trouble II

Like many other matters, our concept and perception of trouble is often flawed. Think of the passengers who were late for their connecting flight—a major inconvenience. But the flight they missed crashed with no survivors. I hate late, but not in this case. What looked and felt like trouble proved to be a blessing. Think of the young man whose love-of-the-moment dumped him, causing major pain and issues with self-worth. But once he finds the love-of-his-life, what seemed like trouble turns out to be a huge blessing. In the moment, we often lack the perspective needed to differentiate trouble from blessing.

1 Kings 18:17 contains the infamous quote from evil King Ahab to Elijah the prophet, "Is it you, you troubler of Israel?" Elijah rightly turned Ahab's words back on him: "I have not troubled Israel, but you have and your father's house, because you have abandoned the commandments of the Lord and have followed the Baals." Elijah had troubled Ahab. Only from Ahab's misguided perspective had the prophet harmed the nation.

Misguided perspectives and trouble are close companions. Think of Jephthah in Judges 11:35. Jephthah had made an infamously foolish vow to make a burnt sacrifice of whatever first came out of the doors of his house to greet him. While he created his own trouble, his words to his daughter were, "Alas, my daughter! You have brought me very low, and you have become the cause of great trouble to me. For I have opened my mouth to the Lord, and cannot take back my vow." Had he known the words of Leviticus 5:4–6. he would have had an honorable solution. In selfish ignorance, he compounded his error by insulting the daughter who was happy to see him come home.

Jephthah stands as a tragic example of Proverbs 29:20: "Do you see a man who is hasty in his words? There is more hope for a fool than for him." Proverbs 21:23 offers the alternative: "Whoever keeps his mouth and his tongue keeps himself out of trouble." When it comes to inviting trouble, few things are more dangerous than foolish words, greed (Prov 15:16), and pride (Prov 16:18). And isn't it amazing how often we find those sins together?

For those who reject pride and serve the Lord faithfully, Scripture offers strong encouragement. "When the righteous cries for help, the Lord hears, and delivers them out of their troubles. The Lord is near to the brokenhearted and saves the crushed in spirit" (Ps 34:17–18). "Blessed is the one who considers the poor. In the day of trouble, the Lord delivers him" (Ps 41:1). "God is our refuge and strength, a very present help in trouble"(Ps 46:1). "… Call upon Me in the day of trouble; I will deliver you, and you shall glorify Me" (Ps 50:15).

Scripture neither denies nor minimizes the troubles faced by the faithful. But Scripture never lets us forget that God always stands with His people.

The Power of Discouragement

And let us not grow weary of doing good, for in due season we will reap if we do not give up. Galatians 6:10

Though it's been years now, I still remember watching the end of a World Cup match between France and Nigeria, pulling for Nigeria for a boatload of reasons. Nigeria had lost a goal on an offsides call, but they were playing the French even. Then there was a mistake by the goalie and the French led 1-nil. The power of discouragement kicked in. After so much effort for so much time, the hearts of the Nigerians fell. You could see it in their faces and their body language.

The power of discouragement is immeasurable. From the Jews who grew thirsty and hungry during the exodus to those who quit building the walls around Jerusalem to those whom the Hebrew writer addressed, we see people giving in to weariness. And we know that the same can happen to us.

In education, it's amazing to hear of people who are ABD—all but dissertation. They've paid boatloads of money and done tons of work, but they can't find a way to complete that final paper. When marriages break, one of the most common explanations is, "I just got so tired that I lost hope." When believers stop serving God, it's not unusual to hear, "I lost my passion; I just wore out."

Discouragement is one of the devil's greatest tools. Obstacles abound, most people choose the easy way, and rewards are seldom instantaneous. That's when the devil offers the obvious temptation: "This is hard; it isn't paying. Why don't you cut your losses by quitting right now?" He never tells the rest of the story; when we cut our losses by quitting, we also surrender all opportunity for gain.

God knows us better than we know ourselves. In the words of Psalm 103:14, "For he knows our frame; he remembers that we are dust." In the words of Proverbs 16:25, "There is a way that seems right to a man, but its end is the way to death." In the very encouraging words of Galatians 6:9, "And let us not grow weary of doing good, for in due season we will reap if we do not give up."

I love both the realism and the optimism of Galatians 6:9. There's a legitimate danger of growing weary even while doing God's good. Admit the danger and expect it. There's no reason to be surprised. Even when doing good to the glory of God, the reward is not always immediate. Few rewards are. Are we willing to trust God enough to let Him decide when the "due season" should come? Haven't we all benefited from delayed rewards? Think of the tomatoes that you grew in your own garden. They're all the sweeter because you nurtured them, waited for them, and anticipated them. Think of that special meal that always takes some extra time, but is always worth every minute.

Our favorite aspect of Galatians 6:9 is the promise that comes at the end: "we will reap, if we do not give up." This is central to God's spiritual reality. No one can steal the reward. No one can deny the blessings that God has in store. The faithful shall reap if they remain faithful. Paul was so certain of this reality that he followed Galatians 6:9 with a huge challenge: "So then, as we have opportunity, let us do good to everyone, and especially to those who are of the household of faith" (Gal 6:10).

When we are tempted toward discouragement, we can revisit the promise of God, we can reaffirm our faith in the goodness of God, and we can open our eyes to the daily opportunities that God puts before us. There's always good that needs doing, and there's always blessing in doing God's good. We do all the good we can for as long as we can and then we hear, "Well done, good and faithful servant…enter into the joy of your master" (Matt 25:21).

I think God means for us to stay too busy, too engaged in and blessed by His great work, to be discouraged. What do you think?

Discouragement Questions

We are afflicted in every way, but not crushed;
perplexed but not driven to despair; struck down, but
not destroyed ... we do not lose heart. ...
2 Corinthians 4:8-9 and 16a

Discouragement is a painful, frustrating, and inevitable part of life. It jumped on Job through stunning loss and was worsened by the efforts of his friends (Job 3 and 6-7). It attacked Moses through the people's grumbling (Exod 17:1-4). It challenged David both through his own sins and through the efforts of his enemies (Ps 27 and 51). It overwhelmed Elijah immediately after his most stunning victory for the Lord (1 Kgs 13). We know it came to Peter after he denied the Lord (Matt 26:69-75). Surely the events cataloged by Paul in 2 Corinthians 11 discouraged him at times. What should these examples mean to us? What should they teach me? At the least, we are reminded that

- discouragement is no respecter of persons. It can attack anyone.
- discouragement is not fatal. It is not stronger than God; it need not be stronger than faith.
- discouragement is unpredictable. It comes at unexpected times and through unexpected means.

- discouragement is not permanent. It may feel never ending, but our minds know better.

What can we do if we fear that we're becoming discouraged? What actions can we take to help ourselves? The following questions can help.

What did I do to get here? Did I play a part in my own discouragement? If so, what has changed? Did I stop praying? Did I fail to let the Word encourage me? Have I backed off from worship? Has my spiritual service decreased? Have I fallen into sin? Have I neglected important relationships or opportunities? Did I have unrealistic expectations of others?

Do I realize that I've been here before? What's similar, and what's different this time? What did I learn last time? How did I escape? What actions helped? What passages strengthened me and invited growth? Who stood with me and blessed my life? What new resources are available now? What might God teach me?

Discouragement will come, but if we stay with God, so will healing. If we stand with God, He will stand with us. As Paul wrote, "So we do not lose heart" (2 Cor 4:16). God renews our inward being. God will raise us up with Jesus. God has eternal plans for us. Our place is at home with God forever. We choose to see with the eyes of faith. We trust God more than we trust ourselves. "So whether we are at home or away, we make it our aim to please him" (2 Cor 5:9). He helps us immeasurably here, and there will be no discouragement in heaven!

Dead Church

There's an abandoned church building adjacent to my brother's farm in south Alabama. A cemetery lies between the building and the road. The steep tin roof is notably stained and rusty. From time to time buzzards—a row of a dozen or so—rest on the ridge of the roof. In one photo, there were also buzzards resting in a leafless tree behind the building. It's quite a sight.

There's something funny about the photo, but it's a dark humor. It drips with irony. If the building were mine, I'd have to tear it down. I wouldn't want the devil using it as a public relations tool.

Sadder still is the notion of a "real church"—people, not a building—dying or being dead. We remember the biblical warnings. If the church in Ephesus didn't repent, Jesus Himself promised, "I will come to you and remove your lampstand from its place" (Rev 2:5). If they stopped being the light, Jesus was unwilling to let them pretend. Jesus promised to personally "war against" false Christians within the church at Pergamos (Rev 2:16). He promised to throw false Christians in Thyatira "onto a sickbed" and "into great tribulation" (Rev 2:22-23). The impenitent in Sardis were promised a surprise visit of judgment (Rev 3:3). And some have described the Laodiceans as the walking dead based on Revelation 3:14ff. Stunning words! They looked shiny and vibrant to human eyes, but Jesus tells us that they were spiritually dead and clueless.

You know there are encouraging threads running through Jesus' letters to the seven churches in Revelation 2-3. Jesus still loved each of those congregations. He was writing to them in love and out of deep concern. Each congregation had the opportunity to repent. None was hopelessly doomed. Most are described as a mixture of the dead and the living, the faithful and the fallen (Rev 3:4).

The Lord affirms that God's judgment remains individual and specific. Even as Jesus had to speak words of warning and correction, He still expressed appreciation for whatever was right with each congregation (Rev 2:2-3, 13, and 19). In each congregation, those who overcame received a rich promise from the Master.

All of us have heard a version of the famous sermon that asks, "If every member of this church gave like I give, how blessed would we be?" (Acts 20:35) "If every member treated others like I treat others, how Christ-like would we be?" (Phil 2:4) "If every member prayed like I pray, would God be pleased?" (Luke 18:1) "If every member loved like I love, would we be who Jesus calls us to be?" (John 13:34-35)

Could we expand the question to ask, "If every member of this congregation were as spiritually healthy as I am, how strong would we be?" Metaphorically, would there be buzzards on the roof? Would the condemnation of Matthew 23:27-28 ring true? Would there be more dead inside the building than in the cemetery?

You know how the devil loves to deceive and misdirect. He'd love for us to turn these thoughts toward judging others. We're far wiser to apply Matthew 7:1-5, John 15:1-17, 2 Corinthians 13:5, Galatians 6:1-5, Hebrews 5:12-6:12, and 2 Peter 1:5-11. We must look first to fix our own faults so we will be better equipped to help others. We must realize that there is no spiritual life and no spiritual fruit outside Christ. We must practice healthy self-examination so that we can have genuine joy in Jesus. While we are blessed to help others all we can, we must be sure that we bear our part of the load.

Above all, we must never stop growing. To stop growing invariably leads to death. In Christ, spiritual growth never ends.

On Wounds

We know the tender and tragic words of Jesus recorded in Matthew 23:37-39. He loved His people and would gladly have spared them the coming destruction. I wonder if they had a clue about the burden that He carried in His heart for them. He knew what was coming (Matthew 24:3-35), and He tried so hard to tell them. But we all know that you can't tell people what they don't want to hear.

I wonder the same about Peter. The words recorded in Matthew 16:23 must have stung: "Get behind me, Satan! You are a hindrance to me. For you are not setting your mind on the things of God, but the things of men." How did Peter hear them? Did he understand their purpose? Did he understand in the moment, or did he need major time to process?

Wounded feelings tend to impede intelligent processing. When angry, we don't think so well. Is this why the text doesn't give us Peter's thoughts and feelings? Is God inviting us to join the story, wrestle with its complexities, and grow from the process?

And what of these stout words from our loving and sacrificial Savior? Jesus couldn't have enjoyed calling one of His chosen an instrument of Satan. Why was He so direct and forceful? To the best of our knowledge, these words weren't public. They were between Jesus and Peter. These words were true. Peter was unwittingly opposing God's plan and asking Jesus to forego His divine mission.

Peter's soul was at stake. One can't work for the devil, either knowingly or not, without great harm and great danger. Jesus loved Peter's soul more than He valued Peter's feelings. We believe this account is in three of the gospels to teach us to imitate our Lord even when our imitation includes risk and pain.

When it comes to the wounds of rebuke, Paul felt this same burden for the Galatians, even to the point of asking them, "Have I then become your enemy by telling you the truth?" (Gal 4:16). We see the same concern and compassion in 2 Corinthians 7:8–12. Paul's rebuke wounded the brethren in Corinth, but causing them pain was not his purpose. He was battling for their souls, putting feelings aside to help them come clean and get right with God. Not all wounds are created equally. We're reminded of Proverbs 27:5–6: "Better is open rebuke than hidden love. Faithful are the wounds of a friend. …" When hearts are right and the truth is spoken in love, Proverbs 28:23 is the result: "He who rebukes a man will afterward find more favor than he who flatters with his tongue."

What we see in the New Testament is a consistent example of valuing truth and righteousness more than feelings. An ethic of love prevails (1 Cor 13, Eph 4:15 and 29–32, 1 Pet 4:8), but never at the expense of truth. We don't see Jesus, Peter, or Paul attacking others to put them in their place or to assert superiority. We do see God's faithful servants willing to tell the truth, even if that truth causes pain.

What do we do when words wound us? I hope we process; I hope we think. Even if spoken without skill, are the words true? Is change needed? Even if the words or the emotions of the speaker are too stout, is there an element of truth? Is there an opportunity to grow, to show grace, to imitate the Lord? We don't need to enjoy our wounds, but better to be wounded than to wound. And it's way better to speak the truth than to fail to love one another.

Self-Inflicted Wounds

It's common enough that we have several phrases for it. "He's his own worst enemy." "He shot himself in the foot." "He couldn't get out of his own way."

My dad likes the TV court shows—*The People's Court, Judge Judy*, and such. During our visits, I watch with him. It's amazing how often one party will have the case won but won't shut up. It's Dad's favorite part of the show—watching a person snatch defeat from the jaws of certain victory.

The Bible speaks of self-inflicted wounds. One sure path to pain is following others into evil. Proverbs 1:10–19 warns us not to consent when sinners entice us. With God's help, we are to foresee their destiny. They think they'll get rich quick with easy pickin's. But Scripture says of them, "… But these men lie in wait for their own blood; they set an ambush for their own lives" (Prov 1:17–18). They don't realize how God has structured reality. As they plot sin, they are plotting the destruction of their own souls (Rom 6:23).

Proverbs 8:32–36 powerfully documents a second sure path to self-inflicted wounds. All who keep God's ways are blessed. Godly wisdom is life-giving. But the one who fails to find and honor wisdom "injures himself, and all who hate me love death" (Prov 8:36). Think of Adam and Even in Genesis 3, and Cain in Genesis 4. Think of virtually the whole world in Genesis 6. Think of David bringing the sword into his own house (2 Sam 12:10). Think of

Solomon following the gods of his wives (1 Kgs 11:4). Think of the Jews who rejected Jesus (Matt 23:37-39).

Proverbs 15:31-32 warns that ignoring instruction and rejecting reproof both lead to self-ruin. "The ear that listens to life-giving reproof will dwell among the wise. Whoever ignores instruction despises himself, but he who listens to reproof gains intelligence."

At some point, all of us have hurt ourselves by ignoring instruction. Think of assembling some Christmas gift—bicycle, tricycle—or assembling a piece of prefab furniture. It's hard to recover from mismatched screws and bolts that were forced into place. Think of ignoring driving directions because we think we know a better way. Ignoring God's instruction carries infinitely more weight.

Scripture offers stunning examples of those who ignored God's commands. Nadab and Abihu died for using "unauthorized fire" (Lev 10). Moses lost access to the promised land for failing to hallow God (Num 20:7-13). Uzzah died on the spot for ignoring God's command (2 Sam 6).

We respect those examples, but we love the Bible's corresponding positive reminders. Repeatedly, we are told of Noah, "Noah did this; he did all that God commanded him" (Gen 6:22, 7:5, and 9). We are reminded of Naaman dipping seven times in the Jordan (2 Kgs 5). He was not cleansed until the seventh dip, until he fully obeyed God. We know where he stood at the sixth immersion. You could easily guess what I believe would have happened had he chosen to dip an eight time. When God specifies, He has spoken.

On a personal level, virtually all of us have been peeved or disappointed by someone who chose to ignore our instructions. If I want the fish sandwich with ONLY mustard, ketchup, and pickle, tartar sauce and lettuce are never a blessing. If you want no starch in the collar, the worker's good intention cannot overcome his bad choice.

Why is it so hard for us to follow instructions, particularly God's instructions? On the softer side, we have an amazing ability to misunderstand. Humans are infamous for failing to pay attention. On the darker side, self-will tempts us all. We can so easily think that we know a better way. Darkest of all, humans just don't like to be told what to do or how to do it. Pride and arrogance invite spiritual destruction (1 Pet 5:5–7).

Dealing with Anger

Anger is a fact of life. Everyone feels anger at some time. Anger is energy; it prepares us for action. Anger is morally neutral, neither good nor bad within itself. How do we know this? God feels anger (Exod 4:14, 25:3-4, and 32:10). God never does anything that is wrong. Jesus showed anger while living on this earth as a human (Mark 3:1-5, John 2:13-17). Jesus never sinned (1 Pet 3:21-23). Also, we have the clear statement of Ephesians 4:26-27, "Be angry and do not sin; do not let the sun go down on your anger, and give no opportunity to the devil."

Ephesians 4:26-27 reminds us that while anger is not sin, it can easily lead to sin. That is true of any strong emotion. These verses also remind us that we are not the slaves of our emotions. Rather, God wills that we be their master. We see this in the case of Cain from Genesis 4:1-8. While Cain was very angry, God did not condemn his anger. Rather, the Lord asked Cain to think about his anger. God asked him, "Why are you angry, and why has your face fallen?" (Gen 4:6) Thinking is one of the very best actions we can take when we are angry. Thinking helps us slow down and avoid rash actions. Thinking gives us occasion to ask ourselves several helpful questions:

- Am I rightly and justly angry?
- Am I angry with the right person and for the right reason?

- Am I projecting anger onto a person when I should be angry at the situation?
- Is my level of anger proportionate to the offense or the danger?
- Am I in control of my anger, or is it beginning to control me?
- Do I realize that no matter how angry I may be, I am still responsible for my words, actions, and attitude?
- What is the godliest action I can take in this moment?

Clearly, there are forms of anger that have no place in the Christian life. Ephesians 4:31 reads, "Let all bitterness and wrath and anger and clamor and slander be put away from you, along with all malice." Colossians 3:8 reads, "But now you must put them all away: anger, wrath, malice, slander, and obscene talk from your mouth." If anger is allowed to grow and deepen, it will lead to many hurtful attitudes and actions.

Being slow to anger is a blessing. Many passages affirm this truth. James 1:19–20 encourages, "Know this, my beloved brothers, let every person be swift to hear, slow to speak, slow to anger, for the anger of man does not produce the righteousness that God requires." Proverbs 14:29 affirms, "Whoever is slow to wrath has great understanding, but he who has a hasty temper exalts folly." Proverbs 16:32 reads, "Whoever is slow to anger is better than the mighty, and he who rules his spirit than he who takes a city." Nahum 1:3 reminds us that the Lord Himself "is slow to anger." Titus 1:7 teaches that an elder in the Lord's church must not be quick-tempered.

In addition to anger itself being a powerful emotion, the actions associated with anger are also a series of learned responses. Most people do not realize that anger raises their blood pressure, increases their heart rate, activates the endocrine system, and prepares them for physical action. Most people do not realize that they have a preferred response to anger. For some, that response is to lash out physically or verbally. For others, it is to burn with pain inside. For some, it is to pray and think before acting. A time-honored approach to dealing with anger is to become aware of the physical changes that anger invites as well as the patterns of behavior that commonly follow anger. Patterns that are unchristian or unproductive can be changed.

One of the wisest ways to deal with anger is to avoid contact with people who stay angry. Proverbs 22:24–25 instructs, "Make no friendship with a man given to anger, nor go with a wrathful man, lest you learn his ways and entangle yourself in a snare." Even if we are unaware of the process, we learn from those around us. We tend to take on their attitudes and to imitate their actions.

In dealing with anger, we need to know that our own actions and attitudes can either limit or incite anger in ourselves and in others. Negatively, Proverbs 25:23 teaches, "The north wind brings forth rain, and a backbiting tongue, angry looks." Positively, Proverbs 15:1 teaches, "A soft answer turns away wrath, but a harsh word stirs up anger." There is an anger cycle. In the negative form, angry thoughts lead to angry words and angry actions, which worsen the angry thoughts. In the positive form, calm and peaceful thoughts lead to calm and peaceful actions, which reinforce the calm and peaceful thoughts.

God can help us find the peace and strength to overcome anger. The Prince of Peace can help us value peacemaking in His name (Matt 5:9, 1 Pet 3:8–12). A daily walk with God with frequent prayer is the best protection from destructive anger.

Ironies

Irony intrigues me. I once saw a Land Cruiser, a large 4-WD SVU that can't be among the most efficient vehicles. On the back panel it said, "V-8." And the tag was a "Protect the Environment" plate. I wonder if the owners recognize the disconnect.

A counseling client once said to me, "All men are such pigs!" Amazingly, she still likes me. Somehow, she gave me a pass from her blanket condemnation. If she knew me better, she'd realize the irony of that choice. On my weaker days, I can oink with the best of them.

A state lawmaker pled guilty to driving under the influence. In light of his guilt, his plea was honest and honorable. But I wonder how many caught the irony of a lawmaker breaking the law in such a dangerous manner.

I'm a notable homebody. I'll drive half the night to sleep in my bed. There's nowhere I'd rather go than home. And one year, I was blessed to make two international teaching trips of more than 28,000 total miles, spending almost a month in Africa.

Occasionally, one of Laura's students will accuse her of acting prejudicially against those of other races. On one occasion, that happened while two South African friends were living with us. I wanted to send them to her school for show-and-tell. I'd also show them photos of the non-Caucasian side of my family. Sadly, some people can't be told or shown.

I've talked with parents who said, "We don't know why our

children are having such problems. We work all the time to give them the best of everything." Maybe the key word is "thing." Their children needed time, teaching, discipline, direction, care, and correction more than they needed things. They longed for love and listening from their mom and dad. Things can never replace relationships.

I love biblical ironies. When Miriam joined Aaron in criticizing Moses for marrying an Ethiopian woman, God struck her with leprosy (Num 12). She spoke against her brother's marriage to a black woman, and God struck her with a disease that makes the decaying skin extra-white. Non-ironically, Moses prayed for her, and God healed her.

Job's friends, who thought Job so sinful and themselves so righteous, were commanded by God to request Job's prayers (Job 42:7-8). Haman was hanged on the gallows he had built for Mordecai (Esth 6:7-9). Daniel's accusers were killed by the very lions to whom they threw Daniel (Dan 6). On a positive note, Abraham showed hospitality to three men, at least two of whom turned out to be angels (Gen 18:1-19:1, Heb 13:2).

"One gives freely yet grows all the richer; another withholds what he should give, and only suffers want" (Prov 11:24). It's both ironic and paradoxical. "Straight math" and earthly accounting principles don't work. In God's economy, the one who gives gains and the one who limits loses. We see the same truth in Proverbs 13:7, "One pretends to be rich, yet has nothing; another pretends to be poor, yet has great riches." Rich and poor can't be adequately defined in terms of financial worth (Matt 16:26, Luke 12:15). Faithfulness counts infinitely more than net worth.

Jesus saw tremendous irony in the church in Laodicea. They said,

"I am rich, I have prospered, and I need nothing …" (Rev 3:17). Jesus ironically corrected them, "… Not realizing that you are wretched, pitiable, poor, blind, and naked" (Rev 3:17). What an error! What a danger! Only God can see us—and help us see ourselves—as we really are. Without God's help, we're walking ironies on the path to doom.

It's Later Than You Think

I was in the office at school trying to finish a job on the afternoon before daylight saving time was to begin. As I began to close things down, I remembered, "This is the evening to spring forward. It's later than I think."

I don't like daylight savings time. More accurately, I don't like springing forward and falling back. I'd be happy with either standard time or savings time; it's the change that bugs me. It bugs me for several reasons. It seems unnecessary; just pick one and stay with it. Time is wasted in changing clocks twice a year. I never remember how to change the various clocks. Twice a year, some forget, making them really early or really late for worship.

The older I get, the more time it seems to take me to adjust to the time change. Though it's only one hour, it throws off my internal clock. It may be that I don't like the fact that we don't have any say-so about the time change. It's mandated from Washington, and they don't ask us what we think. And it may be that I see this biannual change as two changes too many. But it does invite us to think about time.

It's often later than we think. That was true for the people of Noah's day. Remember the words of the Lord: "For as in those days before the flood, they were eating and drinking, marrying and giving in marriage, until the day that Noah entered the ark, and they were unaware until the flood came and swept them all away …" (Matt

24:38–39) Jesus added the warning, "… So will be the coming of the Son of Man" (Matt 24:39). Too late can be deadly.

It was later than the infamous rich foolish farmer thought. He was saying to his soul, "Soul, you have ample goods laid up for many years; relax, eat, drink, be merry" (Luke 12:19). "But God said to him, 'Fool! This night your soul is required of you …" (Luke 12:20). The man had no clue.

According to Daniel 9, it was way later than Belshazzar thought. He was ruler of the greatest empire of his day. He was dining from vessels of gold and silver—vessels which once had been used in the temple of God. By the time Daniel interpreted the handwriting on the wall, God's will was in action. For "that very night, Belshazzar, the Chaldean king, was killed" (Dan 5:30).

Often, it's later than we think in parenting. "Whoever spares the rod hates his son, but he who loves him is diligent to discipline him" (Prov 13:24). Surely diligence includes timeliness. Proverbs 19:18 encourages us not to prematurely conclude that the door of opportunity has closed: "Discipline your son for there is hope. …" Hope, like opportunity, doesn't always last. It presents itself, but quickly disappears if neglected. On the other hand, both hope and opportunity often show amazing resilience, especially when accompanied by faith and prayer.

And it's often later than we think in marriage, in evangelism, and in other important relationships. It may be later than we think in saying thank you, asking advice, or expressing love. What a blessing to do the good that we know to do today (Heb 3:5–15). What a blessing to seize the opportunities God gives, resisting the temptation to think, "I'll do that tomorrow" (Jas 4:13–17).

Closing Another Chapter

Earlier in life, these thoughts would have waited until December to enter my mind. Now, I can find them as early as September when the first taste of fall arrives. Only __ more days to Christmas, and the year ends a week after that.

While every year has its triumphs and its tragedies, its joys and its sorrows, the extremes have seemed more obvious of late—particularly during the pandemic and economic decline of 2020. There's so much that we want to forget or move beyond.

As any year winds down, we're wise to forget the insults and slights that we've perceived. Unless these were matters involving sin, it's wonderful to give people the benefit of the doubt. It's wonderful to give them—and ourselves—a fresh slate for the start of the new year. Of course if sin was involved, the passing of time changes nothing regarding one's spiritual status. Only repentance and God's forgiveness can erase a sin. Matthew 5:21–26, 6:14–15, and 18:15–17 must be honored by those who love God.

As any year winds down, we're wise to forget our disappointments with God. Sometimes, in some respects, our unfounded expectations exceed God's promises. When that's the case, our expectations need adjustment. God is good. God is right. He loves us more than we love ourselves. And He blesses us more than we realize (Rom 5:5–11).

While there's much worth forgetting, there are things that we want to remember—and use—to help us keep growing in Christ. We're wise to remember every good word and every good deed that brethren directed toward us. We're wise to remember that by doing good, they imitated our Lord (Acts 10:38). By doing good, they encouraged us. They challenged us to abound in God's work (1 Cor 15:58). They brought glory to God (Matt 5:16).

We're wise to remember that the end of every year brings extra opportunity for reflection. We're wise to thank God that every new year brings immeasurable opportunity. So many souls need to hear the gospel. So many hurting people need to be comforted. So many good words need to be spoken. So many good deeds need to be done. And in Christ, we are more able than ever to do these good things. In Christ, we can multiply the triumphs and joys of each new year. May God bless us all in the effort!

Closer to Heaven with Each New Year

We all recognize the undeniable fact: Every passing year puts us closer to one of two events, either our departure from this earth (Heb 9:27) or the Lord's return (John 14:3, Acts 1:11). For every faithful Christian, these truths are precious. We eagerly anticipate going home to be with the Lord.

As the calendar turns to a new year, we're wise to pause for reflection. We're wise to ask ourselves, "How can I move closer to heaven during this new year?" We offer the following for your consideration.

We can move closer to heaven by moving closer to Christ. He is "the way and the truth and the life" (John 14:6). No one can come to the Father except through Him (John 14:6, Acts 4:12).

We can move closer to heaven by spending more time with God. We're blessed to notice the priority of worship in heaven (Rev 4). We're blessed to appreciate the fact that the bowls of incense before the throne of God "are the prayers of the saints" (Rev 5:8). Even while we're still on this earth, we're blessed to "serve the Lord with gladness! Come into His presence with singing" (Ps 100:2).

We can move closer to heaven by loving one another more and more. We have always appreciated the way Paul emphasized continual growth of love in 1 Thessalonians 4:9–10. Though they were taught by God to love one another and were practicing that precious love, Paul still urged them to "do this more and more."

Limitless love is one of the abundant blessings of true faith.

We can move closer to heaven by helping others move closer. Preachers have often said, "You can't go to heaven without taking somebody with you" (Matt 18:18–20, Mark 16:15–16). We realize that it may be more accurate to say, "You can't go to heaven without trying to take someone with you." Bottom line, we can't be like Jesus without diligent effort to seek and save the lost (Matt 9:12–13, 10:25, and 18:11).

Why wait until year's end or January 1 to begin moving toward Jesus and heaven?

You Can't Be Too Careful?

Scripture is replete with warnings about human limitations. Jeremiah 10:23 reminds us that "the way of man is not in himself. It is not in man who walks to direct his own steps." Jeremiah 17:9 is darker: "The heart is deceitful above all things, and desperately sick; who can understand it?" Only the Lord can truly know our hearts.

The Proverbs are equally blunt. "There is a way that seems right to a man, but its end is the way to death" (Prov 14:12 and 16:25). "When a man's folly brings his way to ruin, his heart rages against the Lord" (Prov 19:3). "All the ways of a man are pure in his own eyes, but the Lord weighs the spirit" (Prov 16:2 and 21:2).

Though we're blessed with the ability to examine our motives and actions, we lack the perspective and the goodness to do so with complete accuracy. On our good days with God's word in our hearts and with God's help, we often do well. On our bad days, we fail stunningly.

We'll steal and tell ourselves that we're only getting even. Or that we're only paying ourselves what we're really worth. Or no one will know. Or no one will care. And we won't even see the danger we're in.

We'll break our word and tell ourselves, "It's OK because everybody does it." We'll justify breaking faith with God and man while explaining, "It's OK because God really wants me to be happy." We'll do what we know to be wrong and explain to ourselves that life is complicated and things aren't always simple.

We'll think way more highly of ourselves than we ought to think, even taking on titles like "Reverend," "Father," and "priest." We'll explain away the words of Jesus from Matthew 23:9-10. We'll deny the priesthood of all believers from 1 Peter 2:9-10. We'll take up the very role that God condemns in James 2:1-13 and not even realize that we've denied the rich challenge of Matthew 20:25-28.

We'll follow our own wisdom, like the Jews and Greeks of 1 Corinthians 1:18-25, even to the point of rejecting Christ as the very wisdom and power of God. How easily we forget our total lack of standing without Christ. How easily we forget our total dependence on Him.

We know the old line, "You can't be too careful." Spiritually speaking, it's stunningly true. Given the deceitful nature of our hearts, our limited knowledge, and our flawed understanding, we need all the help we can get. We need help from one another (Gal 6:1-2). We need help from God and His word (Ps 119:11). We need direction and correction. We need divine law and divine love. We need grace and guidance. We need God and godly people more than we can ever know.

In this confused and confusing world—at least in the ways described above, we can't be too careful. Souls, including our own, are at stake.

Is there a sense in which people can be too careful? Some see a potential example in Matthew 25: 24-30. At first look, the infamous one-talent servant seems to be too careful. Some assert that he was paralyzed by fear, so afraid of loss that he tried to avoid risk by shirking his duty. Careful reading, however, reminds us that his motivation wasn't primarily fear. The text describes him as "wicked," "slothful," and "worthless." He wasn't overcome by fear in the weight of the moment. Rather, he was both lax in devotion to his master and lazy.

Isaiah 7:10–17 offers a genuine example of a man who was too careful. When the Lord told King Ahaz, "Ask a sign of the Lord your God," Ahaz balked and offered a rationale (Isa 7:11). The rebuke that follows reminds us that there can be no sufficient reason to refuse a direct command of God.

John 12:42–43 offers another example of hyper-caution. Though they believed in Jesus, many—even among the authorities—would not confess him "for fear of the Pharisees." For fear that they would "be put out of the synagogue," they excluded themselves from the coming kingdom of God.

Pilate stands as the consummate example of a man who was too careful. Though he knew Jesus to be an innocent man, he condemned Him to death after the Jewish leaders threatened to question his loyalty to Caesar (John 18:38 and 19:12–13). Pilate let fear and self-interest overcome both conscience and duty (John 19:8–12). In doing so, he guaranteed his status among the weak and infamous.

We can be too careful when we love our pride, our status, our comfort, or even our lives more than we love God, truth, and doing right.

Errors

James 3:2 couldn't be more true. "For we all stumble in many ways. ..." Whenever we forget this truth, life has a way of reminding us.

I have "sent" emails without remembering to hit send and been frustrated because there was no reply. I have deleted files that I needed and had no desire to lose. I have looked for buildings on streets where they have never been located. I have looked for my COVID mask while it was in my pocket. Twice, I have looked for my glasses while wearing them. Thankfully, I have not yet looked for my phone while talking on it, but that day may come.

And these are just "stumbles" that I remember and am willing to admit. What else belongs on the list? To pose a better question, what should I do in light of my frequent errors? What attitudes should an error-prone person should cultivate? Here's the beginning of my list.

Since I have made and continue to make errors, I need to cultivate an attitude of humility. Since I have been wrong many times, I need to realize that I might be wrong this time, too (1 Pet 5:5–7).

Since I have made and continue to make errors, I need to cultivate an attitude of patience and forgiveness toward the errors of others (Matt 6:12–13 and 7:12).

Since I have made and continue to make errors, I need to cultivate an attitude of "correctability." It's bad enough to be wrong, but it's far worse to stay wrong (1 Sam 13 and 15). Given strong biblical warnings, there's no excuse for persisting in disobedience and being destroyed by pride.

Since I have made and continue to make errors, I need to cultivate an attitude of calm and peace. I can't rightly blow up at others for being just as human as I am (Rom 12:18 and 14:19, 1 Cor 13:4–8a).

Since I have made and continue to make errors, I need to cultivate an attitude of awe and respect for the God who is eternally errorless. He never misunderstands. He never misjudges. He never makes a mistake. He consistently treats us better than we deserve and calls us to be better than we are (Rom 5:8, Titus 2:11–14).

Many errors don't destroy relationships or souls, but persisting in error can destroy both. We dare not deny, excuse, or persist in any error.

Unfathomable

There are many things that I'm glad I can't understand. Historically, I can't fathom shooting down a civilian airliner and refusing full access to the crash site, delaying the release of bodies to the next of kin, and withholding the black boxes that might provide answers. I also can't fathom expecting answers that no black box could ever provide.

I can't fathom kidnapping and murdering children because you hate their ethnicity and beating other teens to death in retaliation. I can't grasp lobbing missiles into a neighboring nation that's superior in arms and numbers and doing so from residential areas. I can't wrap my mind around claiming surprise when escalation ensues, when violence is met with violence.

I find unfathomable story after story of pedophile teachers and pedophile religious workers. How could anyone use a precious child in such a way? And some would defend at least some of that activity as consensual, private, and none of our business. Protecting the innocent must be everybody's business.

I find myself perplexed by reports of employee theft by misuse of credit cards and/or illegally writing checks. Don't they know Numbers 32:23b has time-honored, broad, and far-reaching application? Even if people get away with sin or crime from a legal perspective, the costs are extreme. Anyone who will steal with you will steal from you. Anybody who will cheat with you will cheat on you. How can the non-trustworthy ever trust anybody?

To be fair, we should also ask, "As consistent and good as God is, how does anybody choose to defy or disappoint Him?" This one falls far closer to home. We're not thinking of murder, harming a child, or committing another felony, but all—including each of us—sin and fall short of God's glory (Rom 3:23). And 1 John 1:5–10 makes it clear that we don't get everything right even when we come to know and trust Jesus.

I know we're weak, and we ought to be stronger. I know we're ignorant, and we ought to know more. I know we're easily influenced, and we ought to be more stable and consistent. But the extent of our frailty is unfathomable. For creatures made in the image of God, our weakness, bad judgment, and tendency to self-will is stunning. And none of us is immune.

What are we to do in light of our tendency toward evil and the far-reaching influence of this sin-damaged world?

- Pray like our lives depend on God's help (Mark 9:24, Luke 18:13, Jas 1:5).
- Refuse to deny, excuse, or sugarcoat personal sin (1 Sam 12:13, Ps 51).
- Consistently confess and turn from sin (1 John 1:9).
- Trust the cleansing blood of Jesus (1 John 2:1–2).
- Help others come to know and trust the cleansing blood of Jesus (Col 1:13–14).
- Make it our life's aim to walk in the light with Jesus (1 John 1:7).
- Thank God every day for His guidance, challenge, mercy, and grace (1 Thess 5:18).
- Eagerly anticipate our ultimate home where there will be no

sin, doubt, frailty, confusion, or temptation (Rev 21:1–5).

Knowing what we know of life, sin, Scripture, judgment, and grace, to choose any other path is truly unfathomable.

Sadness

Train up a child in the way he should go; even when he is old he will not depart from it. Proverbs 22:6

A man without self-control is like a city broken into and left without walls. Proverbs 25:28

The rod and reproof give wisdom, but a child left to himself brings shame to his mother. Proverbs 29:15

Discipline your son, and he will give you rest; he will give delight to your heart. Proverbs 29:17

Laura and I hated seeing Proverbs 25:28 and 29:15 in action. The sadness was stunning. Mom and grandmother had taken the little boy to dinner. He might have been four years old. He couldn't sit still. He couldn't be quiet. He didn't have an inside voice. And, to the best of our observation, neither Mom nor Granny tried to teach him better.

We know there could be way more to the story than we observed. Perhaps there were medical conditions. Perhaps they had been working with the boy diligently and were giving themselves a short break. We know that we can't see hearts or judge motives.

At the same time, I thought of a phrase from my childhood. I fear that these adults were *raising their own pain* as they failed to correct and control this child. As a teacher, Laura anticipated the challenges of having this damaged kid as a student one day.

We found ourselves wondering. For how many generations has this pattern been repeating? How many parents within this family have chosen the same sad path? Do they know that better options exist? Do they have the blessing of a church family? Are they giving themselves the opportunity to learn better? Like the rest of us, they're going to need all the help they can get as they work to civilize the boy.

I know we weren't perfect parents. I don't even know how many opportunities I missed or how many situations I mishandled. But I also know that we tried. I'm glad we know that we tried. Failing to try would bring immeasurable regret.

Life is a challenge. Rearing children is a challenge. We all need all the help we can find. And we all need to offer all the help that we can. The sooner we start, the better. The more consistent our words and actions, the better. With children, we're constantly on the clock. There's so much to accomplish, so little time, and so much at stake.

Suicide: A Stunning Tragedy

Yet another report of suicide—this time it might be a teen, a young professional, or a senior citizen. We always hope it isn't so. Maybe there was a terrible accident and the authorities got it wrong. Our hearts go out to the families and friends of the deceased.

From a preventive perspective, good people frequently wonder, "Why didn't I see this coming?" "What could I have done to prevent it?' And simply, "Why did this happen?"

Often there are indicators of suicidal ideation. People will talk about ending their lives. They may "put their affairs in order." Sometimes they give away prized possessions, say their good byes, or research suicide methods on the internet. We dare not ignore such signs. But sometimes there are no signs.

When we see "signs" that scare us, love compels us to act. Sometimes it's wise and courageous to ask, "Are you thinking about harming yourself?" Sometimes it's better to help the person connect with medical or mental health professionals. It's always proper to increase our love and support. To borrow and tweak familiar language, "When you see something that's scary or unsettling, say something."

We commonly tell those who are hurting over a friend's suicide, "Please remember that you can never know all that's going on inside another person's head." Only the Lord has such knowledge. Ultimately, we cannot control the actions of others. Those words are true, but they don't provide much comfort.

Some have described suicide as "a permanent solution to a temporary problem." Others suggest that suicide becomes an option when the pain of living exceeds the fear of dying. We want to be very careful with clichés and truisms. For Christians, suicide is never a valid option. Respect for life and the Giver of life preclude it.

Partly in an effort to prevent suicide, some have unwisely asserted, "Suicide is self-murder. Murderers fall under biblical condemnation. Therefore, all who commit suicide are excluded from heaven." While scripture forbids murder and teaches the reality of God's righteous judgment, there is a flaw of omission in this assertion. It fails to consider the victim's mental state. Only the competent can be responsible and culpable for their actions. The assertion also contains a theological flaw. Judgment belongs to the all-knowing and all-loving God (1 Cor 4:1–5, 2 Cor 5:10). It's unsafe, unwise, and harmful to say more than we know.

What can we do to stem the tide of the stunning tragedy of suicide?

- Affirm that life is a precious gift from God (Gen 2:26–27 and 4:1, Acts 17:24–28).
- Love people, especially hurting people, with the love of the Lord (1 Cor 13).
- Never joke about or make light of suicide or depression (Col 4:5–6).
- Especially with hurting people, do the good we know to do (Jas 1:22–24, 2:14–17, and 4:17).
- Pray for all, especially those who are obviously troubled and burdened (1 Tim 2:1).
- Offer comfort and support (Rom 12:15, 2 Cor 1:3–4).

- Treat all with dignity and respect (Matt 7:12).
- Even when we don't know what to say, show up and show love (Eccl 3:7, Job 2:11–13).
- Don't try to explain the inexplicable (Eccl 3:7, Rom 12:3).
- Respect people's feelings. Allow them to voice their feelings without reproach (Eccl 3:7, John 13:34–35).
- Ask for help from God and from others (Jas 1:5). God often blesses through human hands.

When People Don't Want Help

I mean no offense, but I've typed it the way I first heard it: "You can always tell a man from Texas, but you can't tell him much." If that's true, we're all from Texas at times. There's no way to tell people what they don't want to hear.

Have you ever tried to tell a friend, "You're being way too loud and pushy"? "People can't hear your facts because of your attitude and approach. Please chill." It almost never works. People can always miss the point if they want to miss it.

Have you ever tried to tell a friend, "This situation is more nuanced and complicated than you realize"? "Please take a step back and think more before you sound off." Those who are certain of their understanding can be bold to the point of stubbornness. Asking them to think can come across as an attack on reason and an insult to their intelligence. Worse, it can be perceived as an attack on their character.

The old counselor joke goes like this: How many counselors does it take to change a light bulb? Answer: Only one, but the bulb must really want to change. Sadly, it isn't just a joke. Noah was a preacher of righteousness for 120 years, but people didn't want to hear or to change. Isaiah and Jeremiah pled, preached, and prophesied, but the people of their day wanted no help. Though all Jerusalem and Judea heard John, believed, and were baptized, the Jewish leaders resisted and "rejected the purpose of God for themselves" (Luke 7:29–30).

Even Jesus could not help those who refused His help (Matt 19:16–30 and 23:37–39). Even the Son of God could not tell them what they didn't want to hear.

Jesus also encountered this with Peter: "Though they all fall away because of You, I will never fall away" (Matt 26:33). Jesus responded, "Truly I tell you that this very night, before the rooster crows, you will deny me three times" (Matt 26:34). And you know Peter's retort: "Even if I must die with you, I will not deny you!" (Matt 26:35) I don't think he meant to call Jesus a liar, but he deemed Jesus' prophecy to be false. Because he could not believe Jesus' words, there was no plea for prayer and no request for help. It never occurred to Peter that he needed immediate help from God.

I have been Peter. In those times, I never recognized the pride when I said in my heart, "I got this," or "Who are you to tell me what to do?" I was both utterly clueless and half a step from an embarrassing fall. Not only unwilling to hear and be helped, I actually resented that friends were trying to protect me from myself.

All of us have been Peter, and all of us have encountered him. Knowing that, three prayers seem wise.

> *Lord, help us to learn from those times and listen better. Help us not to judge the motives of people who try to help us. Help us to learn what we need to learn to be holy.*
>
> *Lord, help us not to give up. It's so tempting to let the pain of rejection make us quit trying to help others. We know the wicked hurt of having our motives impugned and being kicked for doing good. We know the devil loves to use that pain against us.*
>
> *Lord, help us be less sure of self and more sure of You. You work in mysterious ways, through both success and failure, to help us grow up. We so need Your help. In Jesus' name, amen.*

Pursue Peace

So flee youthful passions, and pursue righteousness, faith, love, and peace along with those who call on the Lord from a pure heart. 2 Timothy 2:22

In the text above, there's a choice and a contrast. We can either chase youthful lusts or pursue the noble and spiritual opportunities that God provides. I don't see how a person could do both. It's not possible to serve two masters (Matt 6:24). Lust and purity stand in stark contrast. Human resources are finite. No one can move in two spiritual directions at once. A choice must be made.

Even when we're talking about people who share our precious faith, peace must be both prized and pursued. The devil is the master of division. He will use the least of matters—even preferences and opinions—to distract and distance us from one another. As brethren, we consciously and persistently pursue peace with one another. We actively and proactively look for ways to get along, to see the good, and to encourage one another.

We know why we need unity with those who "call on the Lord from a pure heart." It answers the prayer of John 17 and follows the teaching of John 13:34–35. It puts us closer to people of faith and courage. It puts us with people who show us God's best, expect God's best from us, and challenge us when we give God less than our best.

How do we identify "those who call on the Lord from a pure heart"? They have no hidden agendas. What we see is real. They don't act out of selfish ambition or conceit (Phil 2:1-4). They consistently act in the best interests of others. They keep their speech and conduct pure (Eph 5:1-21). They manifest the fruit of the Spirit (Gal 5:22-26). According to Scripture, they also "have nothing to do with foolish, ignorant controversies;" they are not quarrelsome; they are "kind to all, able to teach," and patient (2 Tim 2:23-26). They manifest humility even as they correct those who need godly correction. It's not about them—their rights or their feelings. It's always about the Lord's will and glory (Matt 6:33).

Of course it would be unthinkable to pursue peace "along with those who call on the Lord from a pure heart" while failing to call on the Lord in just that manner ourselves. We know how blessed we are to be people of prayer. Knowing that God always hears and always cares fills our hearts with hope and love. Because God always hears and always cares, we are never powerless and never alone.

Many Bibles link 2 Timothy 2:22 with 1 Timothy 6:11-12. It's a helpful and logical linkage. We know the adage, "Be careful what you pray for; you might get it." It's equally true that we should be careful what we pursue; we might catch it. To "catch" righteousness, godliness, faith, love, patience, and gentleness is to draw near to God. It is, in the words of 1 Timothy 6:12, "to fight the good fight of the faith [and] take hold of the eternal life. …"

Think of the precious people who have prayed for us most and best. Remembering them warms our hearts and stirs us to love and good works. It's a cycle of spiritual victory and blessing.

Waste Not

There was a rich man who had a manager, and charges were brought to him that this man was wasting his possessions. Luke 16:1

No wonder the rich man in Jesus' story called his steward to give account. It doesn't surprise us that he planned to fire him. Wastefulness meets strong disapproval even in the eyes of the world. Imagine how it must anger God!

Wastefulness is far more common than we realize. Regrettably, we often limit our thinking to carelessness with food or money. These are legitimate concerns. Jesus ordered the fragments collected after feeding the 5,000, "that nothing may be lost" (John 6:12). "The earth is the Lord's, and all its fullness, the world and those who dwell therein" (Ps 24:1). We are stewards of God's creation, obligated to appreciate His resources. We remember the biblical principle: "Moreover it is required of stewards that they be found trustworthy" (1 Cor 4:2).

Because we are stewards of the time, talent, relationships, and opportunities that God gives, wastefulness in any of those areas is also serious. Jesus had a sense of urgency in doing God's work (Luke 2:49, John 9:4). Paul reminded Titus to urge other Christians "to be ready for every good work" (Titus 3:1). He reminds all of us, "So then, as we have opportunity, let us do good to everyone …" (Gal

6:10). He reminds us to do our part for the effective working and growth of the body of Christ (Eph 4:16). Those reminders oppose our neglect of any gift that God provides.

Wastefulness is more dangerous than we realize. Squandering money doesn't merely invite financial problems; it diminishes self-control and self-respect. It causes people to question our judgment and maturity. Wasting time and talent doesn't just limit knowledge and effectiveness; it stifles growth and zeal for God. Wasting opportunities doesn't just close doors; it violates both the word of God and the spirit of gratitude which should fill our lives (Gal 6:9, Phil 3:17 and 4:9, Col 3:23–24, 1Tim 4:12–16).

The parable of the prodigal son reminds us that wasteful and faithful cannot describe the same person (Luke 16). The parable of the talents reminds us that God does not appreciate those who are lazy and unprofitable (Matt 25). Wastefulness disrespects God, squanders opportunities, and invites others to do the same. It diminishes our character and our influence for good.

From my youth, I remember the tagline of a pork processing plant: "We use everything but the squeal." The plant invited workers to take pride—the right kind of pride—in maximizing productivity and eliminating wastefulness. We remember the pro-education advertising campaign that said, "A mind is a terrible thing to waste." Any gift from God is a terrible thing to waste.

From the military to athletics, we hear people urging, "Be all that you can be!" That sentiment strongly implies, "Waste not! Effectively use every resource at your disposal." We appreciate reminders of the benefits of giving our best and using what's put before us. Nothing is more noble than giving our best to and doing our best for the God who loves and saves us.

Good Miss

Remind them to be submissive to rulers and authorities, to be obedient, to be ready for every good work, to speak evil of no one, to avoid quarreling, to be gentle, and to show perfect courtesy toward all people. Titus 3:1–2

But when the archangel Michael, in contending with the devil, was disputing about the body of Moses, he did not presume to pronounce a blasphemous judgment, but said, "The Lord rebuke you!" Jude 9

Without exception, I'm glad when an election cycle has come and gone. I'll miss the political commercials, but it will be a good miss. The negativity grows increasingly stunning. So many of the attacks are less than honest. So many are unnecessarily and unhelpfully personal. They feel wrong. They feel petty. As much as we value the privilege of voting, they leave us thinking, "There has to be a better way! Surely, we're better than this."

As Christians, we must be better than this. According to God's Word, there is a better way. But it remains a constant challenge to be better than the culture in which we live.

How can we encourage ourselves to guard our tongues against evil speaking and reviling accusation? How can we remind ourselves to live up to the standard set by God? The following commitments have helped me.

Pray daily for those who oppose us. Prayer is the friend of love and the enemy of hate. It would be the height of inconsistency to bless in prayer and to revile in speech (Jas 3:9–12).

Acknowledge the good qualities of those who oppose us. Even a stopped clock is right twice a day. In that every person is made in the image of God, no one totally lacks good qualities (Acts 17:26).

Respect the position of one in authority, even if the person who fills that position has major flaws. Paul did so as recorded in Acts 23:1–5 and in Acts 26. David showed respect to Saul as "the Lord's anointed" (1 Sam 24:6 and 26:7–12).

Appreciate the element of surprise. Sometimes, it's disarming to avoid conflict when conflict is exactly what's expected. It's part of being "wise as serpents and innocent as doves" (Matt 10:16). Jesus did this in complimenting the centurion (Matt 8:10) and the Samaritan (Luke 17:11–19). He did so by teaching the tax collectors and sinners in Luke 15. Being attacked need not make us attackers.

When correction is needed, say what needs to be said clearly, courageously, and lovingly. Jesus stunningly exemplifies this in Matthew 23. The correctives are blunt, but they are followed by words and actions of heartfelt concern. Ultimately, they were followed by the cross and the offer of salvation as recorded in Acts 2. Jesus perfectly embodied the wondrous truth: "Love never ends" (1 Cor 13:8)!

Signs that Faith Is Slipping

Therefore we must pay much closer attention to what we have heard, lest we drift away from it. Hebrews 12:1

Drifting isn't just possible; it's a major, constant, and common danger. I once read a list entitled "10 Signs Your Christianity Has Become Too Comfortable." It made me think, and it invited me to work on a list of my own. It grew into "Ten Signs That Faith Is Slipping."

10. I don't want to be challenged to grow, think, or serve (2 Pet 1:5–11).

9. Before acting, I no longer ask, "Is this right? Will it honor God?" (Prov 20:25, Eccl 5:2, Jas 1:5)

8. I want what I want, and I don't really care how that affects others (Rom 14:7–13, Phil 2:3–4).

7. I see people in terms of their function (what they can do for me or how they complicate my life) rather than as souls made in God's image (Gen 1:26–27, John 3:16–17).

6. My language has been more "earthy," and my conscience is okay

with that (Eph 5:1–7).

5. Giving is a good idea if I feel like it, but it's not part of who I am (Matt 20:25–28).

4. Worshiping with the saints is increasingly optional (John 4:23–24).

3. The Bible, if I read it, tells me what others ought to be and do (Matt 7:21–27, Jas 1:21–27).

2. Prayer is cold or robotic rather than robust and intimate (Luke 22:44, Jas 5:16).

1. The truth of Romans 5:6–8, especially "God shows His own love toward us, in that while we were still sinners Christ died for us," no longer moves me to humility, gratitude, and commitment.

Protection

And do not fear those who kill the body but cannot kill the soul. Rather fear him who can destroy both soul and body in hell. Matthew 10:28

It has happened numerous times in recent years; news outlets are reporting record gun sales. Some attribute this to talk of gun control legislation. Others attribute it to increasing crime rates, particularly armed robberies and home invasions. Others link it to the general decline in civility and respect for life. Whatever the cause, people seem to saying, "We need more protection."

In many respects, protection is good and desirable. We vaccinate our children and get flu shots ourselves. We move investments from volatile stocks to instruments that seem safer. Our church buildings—and buses—have alarm systems. Many congregations have security cameras and security plans. Many of us have as much insurance as we think we can afford. And on our wiser days, still we realize that only God provides protection on the most important level.

Some have viewed God's protection unbiblically and illogically. Joab thought he could protect himself by holding onto the horns of the altar (1 Kgs 2:28-35). The evil people of Isaiah's day sought to replace God's protection with military alliances. Isaiah 31:1 says of them, "Woe to those who go down to Egypt for help and rely on horses, who trust in chariots because they are many, and in horsemen because they are very strong, but do not look to the Holy One of Israel or consult the Lord!" The evil people of Jeremiah's day thought that having the temple of the Lord protected them (Jer 7:4). False prophets gave false comfort, "Saying, 'Peace, peace!' when there is no peace" (Jer 6:14 and 8:11). Isaiah 48:22 and 57:21 speak definitively: "'There is no peace,' says my God, 'for the wicked.'" There is no peace, and there is no protection.

On the other hand, God promises protection for the faithful. "Fear not, Abram. I am your shield, your reward shall be very great" (Gen 15:1). Proverbs 30:5 affirms, "Every word of God is proven true; he is a shield to those who take refuge in Him." In times of deep trouble, David said to God, "But You, O Lord, are a shield about me, my glory and the lifter of my head" (Ps 3:3). Psalm 84:11 extols, "For the Lord God is a sun and shield; the Lord bestows favor and honor. No good thing does he withhold from those who walk uprightly." Psalm 119:113–120 contrasts the double-minded with those who love God's law. The passage praises God as a shield to those who hope in His word, keep His commandments, observe His statutes, and reject evildoers.

God's protection is not automatic; He links it to our faithfulness. In fact, He promises to oppose those who oppose Him. God's protection is not always physical as countless martyrs can attest. Hebrew Christians, under God's protection, had their property plundered (Heb 10:34). But faith led them to joyfully accept that loss. They knew what we need to know, that we have "an enduring possession" in heaven. Ultimate protection is spiritual protection (Rom 8:31–39). Nothing matters as much or as long.

Lucky Day

June 7, 2007, was supposed to be one of the luckiest days ever. The media declared it so. After all, it was it was 07/07/07 What could be luckier than three sevens?

I've never been much of a believer in luck, whether good or bad. When I see a rabbit's foot on a keychain, it invites me to think that the rabbit wasn't so lucky. I've stepped on many cracks, but my mother's back seems to be OK most of the time. Whenever a black cat crosses my path, I don't think of bad luck. My first thought is, "I'm really happy that Laura doesn't have a cat."

As a concept, luck is so easily abused. When we label an outcome "bad luck," we tend to avoid honest assessment and personal accountability. We don't consider the possibility of a connection between our conduct and the event. When we label an outcome "good luck," we tend to forget that "every good gift and perfect gift is from above, coming down from the Father of lights …" (Jas 1:17). We tend to downplay our dependence on God. We fail to give God both credit and thanks for every blessing.

Rather than believing in and working to invite good luck, it seems far wiser to believe in the blessings of sound values, clean living, and hard work. Rather than believing in fate, it makes far more sense to believe in a loving God who blesses us every day. Certainly, bad things happen to good people, and God extends many blessings to every person. Still, the evidence of Scripture clearly supports strong confidence in the goodness, power, and providence of God to care for His children.

Isn't it interesting that we find absolutely no teaching regarding luck in the Bible? When Eve had a son, she didn't say, "This is my lucky day." Rather, she acknowledged her son as a gift from God (Genesis 4:1 and 25). Joseph didn't credit luck for his rise to power in Egypt. He saw his elevation as part of God's plan to save His chosen people (Gen 50:20). Paul didn't credit his conversion and apostleship to luck. He saw both as powerful manifestations of God's grace (Phil 3).

It is my conviction that we would be wise to avoid the language of luck. Our language both reflects and affects our thinking. When any blessing comes, we want our first thoughts to be, "Thank You, Lord, for being good to us again. How can we use this blessing to glorify Your name?" When any challenge comes, there can be no better thoughts than, "Lord, help us through this. Help us learn to trust You more. Make us more like You." That's biblical thinking. That's biblical language. That's the language of faith.

Doing Good

If you know these things, blessed are you if you do them. John 13:17

We need to do what we know to be good, true, and right. God made us that way. Something within us says, "You should!" Something within us says, "You must!" Something within us says, "If you don't, you'll be sorry." And something within us should be taught to say, "If you do, you will be blessed." We need to believe what the good book teaches.

Doing good strengthens us. It gives us all the more reason to pray. It allies us with other faithful souls. It affirms our trust in God. It helps us learn to overcome fear, weakness, and opposition (1 Cor 15:58).

Doing good enables us. God gives more resources and more opportunities to those who faithfully use what they currently have (Matt 25:21 and 23). It is by doing the good we know to do, "by reason of use" that our "senses are exercised to discern both good and evil" (Heb 5:13-14). By doing the good we know to do, we learn to choose between better and best, we learn to "walk in a manner worthy of the Lord, fully pleasing to him, bearing fruit in every good work, and increasing in the knowledge of God (Col 1:9-10. Eph 4:1, 1 Thess 2:12).

Doing good identifies us. It identifies us as caring, giving, and loving followers of Christ. We love Luke's synopsis of the gospel that bears his name: "In the first book, O Theophilus, I have dealt with all that Jesus began **to do** and to teach" (Acts 1:1). We love Peter's description of Jesus as one who "went about doing good" (Acts 10:38).

Doing good blesses us. We've read that from John 13:17. Doing good in the name of Jesus blesses us with a sense of purpose and noble mission (Matt 28:18–20, Luke 19:10, Col 4:12–13). It blesses us with assurance of ultimate victory (1 Cor 15:53–58). Doing good blesses us with happiness, the real and lasting kind.

What a joy to do what we know to be good, true, and right to the glory of God!

Blessings of Evangelism

Go therefore and make disciples of all nations, baptizing them in the name of the Father and of the Son and of the Holy Spirit. ... Matthew 28:19

As we share the gospel of Jesus Christ, we recognize and honor His authority (Matt 28:18). As we share the gospel of Jesus Christ, the Lord has promised to be with us (Matt 28:20). We love to read the Great Commission as both commandment and opportunity. It's amazing how many doors open as we teach the soul-saving good news of the risen Christ.

As we evangelize, we find ourselves more appreciative of our elders. 1 Timothy 3:2 describes elders as "able to teach." While this does not imply that every elder must be a public speaker (1 Tim 5:17), elders have the experience and the willingness to take advantage of teaching opportunities. Their wisdom and examples encourage us as we step out in faith to bless others with the gospel. They give us strong hope that those who obey the gospel will be fed and protected by the word.

As we teach the good news, we find ourselves more appreciative of our preachers. People who are teaching their neighbors listen to sermons with diligent attention. Every sermon could contain both information and encouragement that will assist in the saving of a soul. We know that all conversions are team efforts, with God leading the team (1 Cor 3:5–6).

As we evangelize, we find ourselves more appreciative of our parents—provided that those parents were godly (2 Tim 1:3–5 and 3:14–17). For most of us, faith began and was nurtured at home (Eph 6:1–4, 2 Tim 1:5 and 3:14–17). For those whose biological parents were not Christians, there is so often a spiritual father or mother through whom God sent His blessings.

As we tell the sweet story of Jesus, we find ourselves more appreciative of our Bible teachers. 2 Timothy 2:15 applies to all types of Bible learning, but most of us remember special teachers who helped our parents lay a most excellent foundation. Bringing those with whom we are studying to a happy, vibrant Bible class is a genuine pleasure.

As we evangelize, we find ourselves more appreciative of the fellowship of the church. We want potential Christians to meet God's family and to see how we love one another (John 13:34–35, Eph 4:29–32, Phil 2:1–4). At a heightened level, we appreciate the prayers of brethren that we won't "grow weary while doing good" (Gal 6:9).

As we invite others to share in God's grace, we will find ourselves more appreciative of the privilege of prayer. We'll remember Jesus' call to evangelistic prayer (Matt 9:37–38). We'll better understand Paul's call to prayer in support of evangelism (1 Tim 2:1–10).

As we evangelize, we will find ourselves more careful with and more appreciative of our own examples. It is by seeing the good works of Christians that many first come to give glory to God (Matt 5:16). Even as God calls us to be salt and light, the world loves to label Christians as judgmental hypocrites. The power of a Christlike example does so much to counter the world's false label (1 Tim 4:12–16). With whom will you share the gospel today?

Scripture Index

Old Testament

Genesis
1	182
1:26–27	105, 149, 177, 182, 272
2:18	18
2:26–27	262
3	189, 215, 236
3:1–8	152
3:8	40
3:9	40
3:11	40
3:12	86
3:13	40
4	189, 236
4:1	277
4:1–8	239
4:6	239
4:25	277
6	236
6-8	98
6:5–8	209
6:22	237
7:5	237
7:9	237
12	215
12:1-3	42
12:10–13	42
12:13	89
12:14–20	42
13	42, 189
13:14–16	42
14	42
15	42–43
15:1	275
15:2	38, 42–43
15:4–5	43
15:6	43
16	46
16:4–5	44
16:8	44–45
16:11	46
16:13	46
17:17	89
18:1–19:1	243
20	215
20:2	89
21:15–21	45
22	88

24:2	38	32	189
24:12	39	32:10	239
24:15	39	32:22–25	187
24:26–27	39	**Leviticus**	
24:52	39	5:4–6	224
24:52ff	39	10	237
25:7–8	178	19:18	154
25:22	91	**Numbers**	
27	91, 215	12	186, 243
29	91, 215	12:1–3	187
30	91	16	187
30:8	91	20:7–13	237
31:36–42	91	21	89
32	89	32:23b	256
32:25	92	**Deuteronomy**	
32:28	91–92	4:2	17, 24
32:30	91	6	48
33:4	92	7:2	89
37–50	55	10:12–13	48
39	215	10:13	146
39:1–9	152–153	12:32	17
50:20	277	13:1–5	152, 215
Exodus		13:15	89
4:14	239	20:17	89
4:24–26	89	32	222
5:21	186	**Joshua**	
14:10–12	159	2:8–14	141
14:11	186	7	190
14:12	186	9	36
16:1–3	159	9:8	37
16:2–3	186	9:9–10	37
17:1–4	228	9:14	36
20	138	15:6–15	142
20:15–17a	212	15:11	142
25:3–4	239		

23:14	144	13	89
24:14–15	153	16:5–13	153
24:19–20	2	18:5	152
Judges		18:30	152
4	89	**1 Kings**	
11:29–31	153	2:28–35	274
11:35	223–224	3	142
17:6	94	3:13	142
21:25	94	11:4	237
1 Samuel		13	57, 228
2	187	13:11–22	152
12:13	257	18	71
13	255	18:17	223
13:12	87	19	59, 130
13:13	130	21:29	89
15	189, 255	**2 Kings**	
15:17	130	1	71
15:22–23	130	2:29–31	52
16:7	36–37	5	237
17:28-29	153, 190	21	96
17:39	13	22–23	26
24:6	277	**1 Chronicles**	
25	130	22	161
26:7–12	271	22:1	161
2 Samuel		22:3–4	161
1	189	22:5	162
1:1–16	153	22:5–6	161
6	90, 237	22:7–8	161
7	142	22:9-10	161
7:16	142	22:12	162
11	89	22:17–18	162
11–24	130	22:18	162
12:10	236	22:19	162
12:13	87	**2 Chronicles**	
12:15–23	53		

7:14	26, 51–55	19:14	202
34	89	23	58
Ezra		24:1	268
9:5–9	52	27	228
Nehemiah		27:13	59
4:1–3	215	34:17–18	224
8:1–12	31	41:1	224
Esther		46:1	228
1	21	50:15	224
1:10	22	51	95, 189, 228, 257
3	22	51:3–4	87
3:3	22	55:19	115
4:1–3	215	62:11	131
6:7–9	243	84:11	275
Job		90:7–12	144
1–2	191	100:2	249
2:11–13	263	103	193
3	228	103:14	226
6–7	228	103:15–16	193
30	34	117:2	176
30:20	34	119	2, 21
38	34	119:9–11	94
38:1	34	119:11	252
42:1–6	54	119:26–27	55
42:7–8	243	119:71	222
42:7-9	96	119:89	110
Psalms		119:89–90	116
1	31	119:97	xii
1:2	30	119:105	94
3:3	275	119:105–106	56
15	104, 168, 207	119:113–120	275
15:2	207	133	65
15:4	207	147:5	131
19:7–11	134, 202	**Proverbs**	
		1:10–11	215

1:10–19	236	18:19	219
1:17–18	236	18:21	219
3:5	38	18:22	18
3:5–6	38, 56, 184	19:3	251
3:5–8	148	19:18	246
3:7	38	20:22	152
3:34	52	20:25	153, 272
4:7	152	21:2	94, 251
5:1–6	152	21:5	153
8:32–36	236	21:23	128, 224
8:36	236	22:1	18
10:19–21	202	22:3	152
10:24	53	22:6	140, 259
11:24	243	22:24	18
13:7	243	22:24–25	241
13:15	52, 95	23:13–14	150–151
13:24	151, 246	24:21	116
14:12	251	25:11	201
14:15	152	25:11–12	206
14:29	240	25:21–22	152
14:34	51	25:23	241
15:1	201, 241	25:28	150, 219, 259
15:16	224	26:3–4	202
15:31–32	237	26:4	19
16:2	256	26:5	19
16:18	224	26:18–19	146
16:25	94, 226, 251	26:18–22	206, 219
16:27–30	219	27:2	206
16:28	219	27:5–6	234
16:32	150, 240	28:23	234
17:9	219	29:11	19, 73–74, 128, 151–152, 202, 206, 209
17:15	186		
17:27–28	206	29:15	259
18:6–8	219	29:17	259
18:13	152, 202		

29:20	152, 202, 209, 224	18:15	26
30:5	275	27:9–11	32
30:6	24	27:14–15	32
31	3	36	11
31:26	202, 206	44:4–5	32
Ecclesiastes		**Ezekiel**	
3:7	263	12:2	8–9
5:2	272	18	96
7:1	18	33:1–9	216
9:5	144	**Daniel**	
Isaiah		2:44	110
1	71	3	190
1:18–20	153	3:16–18	54
6:1–5	153	4	149
7:10–17	253	5:30	246
7:11	28, 253	6	190, 243
10:20–27	52	7	88
31:1	274–275	9	246
48:22	275	9:3–11	87
53	88–89, 221	9:3–19	222
53:3	83, 221	**Joel**	
53:7	34–35	2:28	88
57:21	275	**Micah**	
59	41	6:8	25
59:1	41	**Nahum**	
59:1–2	61, 153	1:3	240
59:1–3	92, 98	**Malachi**	
Jeremiah		3:6	116
2:11	116	**New Testament**	
6:14	275	**Matthew**	
6:16	26	1:5–6	142
7:4	275	4	2, 94, 215
8:11	275	4:3	134
10:23	251	4:5–6	49
17:9	251		

Reference	Pages
4:5–7	134
4:6	11, 21, 101
4:8–9	134
5:5	149, 153
5:6	133, 138, 168
5:7	105
5:8	104, 168
5:9	66, 104, 201, 241
5:13	138
5:13–16	183
5:16	16, 19, 135, 164, 248, 281
5:17–20	49
5:21–26	247
5:23–24	203
5:37	208
5:43–48	33, 174, 177
6	79
6:1	16
6:9–13	153
6:12–13	254
6:14–15	247
6:24	61, 266
6:33	267
6:34	199
7	69
7:1	19, 93
7:1–5	6, 94, 140, 231
7:7–12	153
7:12	7, 17, 64, 139, 147, 218, 254, 264
7:13–14	110
7:15	215
7:15–20	69
7:16	69
7:21–23	11, 48, 71, 84, 125
7:21–24	48, 90
7:21–27	24, 273
7:24-27	48
8:10	271
9:10–13	127
9:12–13	250
9:3	127
9:34	127
9:37–38	281
10:1–4	89
10:16	271
10:25	250
10:28	274
10:32–33	25
10:42	135
11:16–19	127
11:28–30	149
12:1–14	127
12:33–37	174
12:34	209
12:35b	220
12:36	209
12:36–37	137, 220
13:9	4
13:19	30
13:51	4
13:57	83
14	190
15	124
15:1–2	49
15:1–9	11
15:3–9	9
16:13–19	27

16:23	233	23:37–39	67, 83, 174, 231, 237, 265
16:24–26	84		
16:25–27	135	24	96
16:26	243	24:3–35	233
17:20	110	24:23–24	215
18:11	250	24:38–39	245–246
18:15	220	24:39	246
18:15–17	7, 140, 247	24:48–50	90
18:15–20	218	25	94, 269
18:18–20	250	25:1–13	184
18:21–35	160	25:21	227, 278
19:1–6	121	25:21–23	183
19:16–30	265	25:23	278
19:30	84	25:24	87
20:16	84	25:24–30	252
20:20–28	153	25:31–46	79, 141
20:25–28	252, 273	25:40	141
21:22	53	25:41–46	96, 125
21:23	24	26–27	89
21:23–27	35, 49	26:33	265
21:24–25	24	26:34	265
22:21	49	26:35	265
22:34–40	174	26:36–42	24
22:34–49	154	26:37–47	53
22:36–40	79	26:51–56	68
22:37–38	61	26:62–63	35
22:39	17, 149	26:69–75	89, 228
22:39–40	147	27	189
23	49, 93, 174, 208, 271	27:13–14	35
23:2	166	28:18	149, 280
23:3	11	28:18–20	79, 135, 140, 279
23:4	11	28:19	183, 280
23:9–10	253	28:20	280

Mark

23:27–28	233
3:1–5	239

4:24	5, 30	11:9–13	76
9:24	257	12:15	243
10	67	12:16–21	28, 153, 191
10:13–16	117	12:19	131, 246
10:14	119	12:20	246
10:21–22	105	12:48	182
10:22	83	13:1–5	33, 97
10:23	18	13:31	89
11:24	53	14:12–14	108
12:30	99	14:25–28	153
12:41–44	142	15	131, 271
14:3–9	142	15:7	101
14:29–30	84	15:10	115
14:32–42	83	15:17–24	152
14:43–45	84	16	269
14:53–59	127	16:1	268
14:66–72	84	16:8	37
16:15	184	16:8b	213
16:15–16	250	17:11–19	184, 271
Luke		18:1	76, 195, 231
2:49	268	18:11–12	87
2:52	115	18:13	257
4:16ff	17	19:10	135, 279
7:29–30	264	22:70–71	127
7:30	57	22:44	273
7:36-50	18	23:34	152, 155
8:18	5–6, 30	23:39–43	59
8:37	83	**John**	
9	71	1:11	83
9:25	125	1:35–51	31
9:53	83	2:13–17	239
9:57–62	153	2:19–21	1
10	33, 71	3:4	1
10:25–37	89, 187	3:16	25, 134
11:9–10	53	3:16–17	272

3:16–21	68	14:1–5	58
3:17	71, 123	14:3	249
3:19–20	9	14:6	90, 122, 125, 221–222, 249
4:10	126		
4:23–24	273	14:9	47
5:39–40	17	14:13	53
6:12	268	15:1–8	90
6:48–59	90	15:1–17	231
6:63	216	15:16	53
6:66	83	16:1–4	53, 84
7:5	83	16:2	187
7:24	19, 188	16:12	35
8:1–11	23, 105	16:23	53
8:24	90, 123, 125	16:33	17, 221–222
8:29	24, 154, 167	17	266
8:31–32	31, 62	17:17	122
8:44	2	17:21	65
9	1	18:33–36	67
9:2	1	18:36	52
9:4	24, 268	18:38	253
9:16	1	19:8–12	253
9:18	1	19:10	131
9:28–29	1	19:11	131
10:10	122	19:12	131
11	59	19:12–13	253
11:22	53	21:20	21
11:35	179	**Acts**	
11:50	187	1:1	165, 279
12:42–43	253	1:11	249
12:48	48	1:15–26	150
13:17	278–279	2	99, 271
13:29	107	2:37–38	62
13:34–35	133, 173, 203, 231, 263, 266, 281	2:38	102
		2:41–47	101
14:1–4	123	2:44–45	107

2:47	52	17:26	271
4:11–12	90	17:28	182
4:12	249	17:30	25
4:13	202	17:32	2
4:19	49	18	149
4:34–37	107	18:24–28	7, 17
4:36–37	142	18:26	2
5	96	18:27–28	29
5:29	49	18:28	51
5:41	155	20:26	216
7:60	155	20:35	72, 107, 231
8:1–3	84	20:35b	107
8:4	79, 160, 183	21	126
8:35–39	101	21:26–29	153
9:23–25	56	23:1–5	150, 271
9:26–27	142	23:11–22	56
10–11	52	26	174, 271
10:34ff	52	**Romans**	
10:38	248, 279	1:7	19
11:19	183	1:13	56
11:20	186	1:16	31, 124–125
11:25–26	142	1:16–17	28
11:26	134	1:17	18
12	57, 96, 131, 149	1:20	47
12:20–24	29	3	168
12:20–25	153	3:23	87, 92, 98, 153, 257
13:1–3	142		
15:36–41	65	5:1–2	61
16:25	159	5:1–5	54, 84
16:30–34	101	5:5–11	247
17:11	1, 7, 30–31, 163, 184	5:6–11	25, 99
		5:6–8	99, 273
17:21	2, 14	5:8	255
17:24	121	5:20	60
17:24–28	262	6	98

6:1	60	13	17, 150
6:4	60–61	13:1–7	49
6:4–5	61	14	105
6:4–6	25	14:7–13	272
6:7–10	61	14:19	104, 255
6:10	61	15:4	17, 51, 153
6:11	60–61	**1 Corinthians**	
6:12	61	1:18–25	252
6:12–14	99	3:5–6	281
6:13	61	3:9	135
6:13-16	61	4:1–5	262
6:14	61	4:2	268
6:17	61	6:1–7	153
6:22	61	7	18
6:23	61, 92, 236	7:8	18
7	189	7:32–33	18
8	58, 192	10:1–13	153
8:1	61	10:11	17
8:28	85	10:12–13	151
8:31–39	85, 200, 275	10:13	49
8:35–39	135	13	7, 58, 65, 149, 234, 262
9–11	52		
10:14–17	28	13:4	178
10:16	100	13:4–5	153
11:22	93	13:4–8	105, 211
12	169	13:4–8a	255
12:1–2	2, 80, 189–190	13:8	271
12:2	157	13:11	117
12:3	28, 94, 170, 263	15:10	170
12:6–21	169	15:12–19	2
12:14	33	15:26	179
12:14–21	76	15:33	18
12:15	73, 262	15:51–58	85
12:17–21	68, 153, 174, 177	15:53–58	279
12:18	66, 104, 174, 255	15:54–58	179

15:57	170	11:22–28	81
15:58	19, 169–170, 187, 248, 278	11:22–33	159
		11:23–28	84
16:15–16	148	11:28–29	200

2 Corinthians

1:3-4	58, 81–82, 95, 262	12	96
1:22	102	12:1–10	95
1:4	82	12:7–10	53, 159
1:5	81	13:5	231
1:7	82		

Galatians

2	102	1:6	115
2:15–16	81	1:8–9	215
3:4–6	82	2:11–21	202
4:1	82	2:13	89
4:2	68	3:26–29	52
4:8–9	228	4:16	174, 202, 204, 234
4:16	81–82, 229	5:16	102
4:16a	228	5:16–26	102
4:17	82	5:22	176
4:18	82	5:22–23	150
5:1	81	5:22–26	105, 267
5:5	102	5:25	102
5:7	55, 82, 198	6:1–2	7, 140, 218, 220, 252
5:9	229	6:1–5	231
5:10	262	6:6	164
5:10–11	93, 125	6:7–9	51
5:16	157	6:9	78, 191, 226, 269, 281
6:10	102	6:10	33, 166, 225–226, 268–269
7:2–12	204		
7:8–12	95, 234		

Ephesians

8:2	107	1:3	171
9:6	108	1:3–12	171
9:6–7	72	1:13	102
9:6–9	172	2	122
11	228		

2:1–3	98	5:4	210
2:1–10	52, 99, 101	5:17	139
2:5	168	5:19	116
2:8–9	19	5:25–29	80
4	103	5:29	174
4:1	278	5:29–30	220
4:7	170	6:1–4	281
4:11–16	110, 117, 164	6:4	140
4:13	168	6:5–9	17
4:14	11	6:10–20	68
4:15	5, 94, 103, 115, 174, 177, 234	6:13	13

Philippians

4:16	269	1	17
4:17	103, 123–124	1:12–18	18
4:18	123	1:19–26	145, 178
4:19	103	2	170
4:21	103	2:1–4	65–66, 110, 149, 154, 169, 201, 267, 281
4:22	103		
4:23	123		
4:24	103	2:3	108
4:25	147, 212, 220	2:3–4	147, 164, 222, 272
4:25–29	103	2:4	108, 231
4:26–27	239	2:8	24
4:27	190	2:9–11	84
4:28	138, 212	2:12–13	19, 113, 168
4:29	86, 128, 147, 152, 164, 201, 209–210, 216, 219–220	2:14	160
		3	277
		3:1–14	153
4:29–31	217	3:7–11	133
4:29–32	169, 174, 234, 281	3:17	269
4:30	102	4:2	64
4:31	86, 210, 240	4:2–3	64–65
4:32	160, 176	4:4–5	198
5:1–7	273	4:4–9	155
5:1–21	267	4:4–10	160

4:6	197	4:9–12	109
4:6–7	58, 76, 197–198	4:13–18	58
4:8	76, 198	4:16	179
4:9	197–198, 275	5:14	222
4:10–12	198	5:15–18	116
4:10–13	198	5:17	76, 164
4:11	199	5:18	257

Colossians

1:9–10	278	5:19	57
1:13	18	5:20–23	222

2 Thessalonians

1:13–14	52, 101, 257	1:3–10	96
1:15–18	121	1:8	57, 100
2:14	17	2:9–12	9, 96
2:20	17	2:11	57
3:1–5	198	2:13–14	29
3:8	240	3:11–12	217

1 Timothy

3:12–17	155	1:8–11	70
3:16	116, 171	1:10	70
3:16–17	2, 30	2:1	262
3:17	17, 24, 61, 164, 171	2:1–4	164
3:23	79	2:1–7	150
3:23–24	61, 190, 269	2:1–10	281
4:5	188	2:2–7	116
4:5–6	262	3:2	280
4:6	5, 128, 210	4:1	69
4:7–15	149	4:11–16	18
4:12–13	279	4:12–16	269, 281

1 Thessalonians

1:2–10	133	5:8	80
1:3	184	5:13	217
1:7	184	5:17	280
1:13	29	6	150
2:12	278	6:7	108
4:9–10	113, 249	6:9–10	18
4:9–11	185	6:11–12	267

6:12	267	2:9–18	222
2 Timothy		3:5–15	246
1:3–5	281	4:12	1
1:5	281	5:5–11	222
1:12	148	5:8	24
2:15	9–11, 14, 21, 48, 94, 163, 281	5:11–6:3	113
		5:12–14	10
2:22	266–270	5:12–6:3	115
2:23–26	267	5:12–6:12	231
2:24–26	127	5:13–14	278
3:5	11	6:6	84
3:7	10	6:10	135, 141
3:14–17	11, 17, 20–21, 28, 51, 88, 281	8:7–13	17
		9:27	144, 249
3:23–26	110	9:27–28	180
4:6–8	159	10:16–25	99
4:9–10	115	10:24	172, 201
4:14	115	10:24–25	79, 163, 216
Titus		10:34	275
1:7	241	11:1–3	120
1:10–16	70	11:6	120
1:13	70	11:24–26	152
1:16	70, 72, 84	11:31	142
2:11	169	11:35–40	190
2:11–14	160, 255	12:1	272
2:11–3:8	169	12:1–11	54, 95, 222
2:13	170	13:2	76, 243
2:14	78	13:5	194
3:1	127, 164, 268	13:7	149
3:1–2	270	13:8	110, 116, 163
3:8	141	13:13	149
3:9	127	13:15	163, 171
Hebrews		13:15–16	135
1:14	76	13:16	163
2:1–4	110	13:17	140

James
1:5	37–38, 55, 257, 263, 272
1:6	37
1:13–15	61
1:17	28, 75–76, 276
1:19–20	205, 240
1:21–27	273
1:22–24	262
1:22–25	101
2:1–13	252
2:14–17	79, 262
3	6, 105, 206
3:1–12	166
3:2	136, 205, 210
3:5–6	174, 206
3:8	210
3:9–12	271
3:17	152
3:18	104
4:6–8	52
4:7–10	150
4:13–17	246
4:14–15	144
4:17	262
5:16	86, 164, 273
5:19–20	135

1 Peter
1:3	171
1:4	171
1:15	139
1:22	19
2:9–10	252
2:13–14	18
2:17	50
2:18–25	54, 160
3:1	18
3:1–6	140
3:8–12	241
3:16	21
3:21–23	239
4:7–11	169–172, 202
4:8	133, 234
4:11	49, 101
4:15	217
4:17	19, 101
5:5	18
5:5–7	58, 150, 238, 254
5:5–11	52, 105
5:6	101, 164
5:8–9	151

2 Peter
1:1–3	171
1:4	17, 171
1:5–7	149
1:5–8	110, 115, 164
1:5–11	113, 150, 231, 272
1:8	185
1:10–11	18
1:12–13	113, 164
1:14–18	69
1:19–21	11, 21, 88
3:10	134
3:14	69
3:14–16	49
3:14–18	2, 11, 94, 101
3:16	10, 14, 19

1 John
1:5–10	257
1:5–2:2	99

1:7	257	2:4–5	27
1:7–10	62	2:5	79, 84, 230
1:8	93	2:8–11	96
1:8–10	87	2:10	190
1:9	86, 257	2:10b	179
2:1–2	164, 257	2:11	179
2:3–6	62	2:12–17	69
2:6	62	2:13	231
2:8–11	62	2:14–16	27
2:15–17	17	2:15–17	69
2:17	62	2:16	52, 84, 230
2:24–25	62	2:19	231
2:28	63	2:22–23	230
3:1–3	47, 62	3:1	27
3:18	62	3:2–3	27
3:19–20	99	3:3	84, 230
3:19–21	63	3:4	27, 231
4	105	3:14–18	84
4:1	117, 152	3:14–22	27
4:4	17	3:14ff	230
4:7	133	3:17	244
4:7–11	174	4	249
4:7–21	62, 66	5:8	249
4:17–18	63	12:10	127
5:11–13	62	14:13	181
5:14–15	63	21:1–3	135
3 John		21:1–5	58, 258
2	137	21:8	215
Jude		21:8b	212
9	270	21:18–19	21
Revelation		22:1–5	58
2–3	231	22:18–19	14, 17, 96
2:1–7	80		
2:2–3	78–79, 231		
2:4	78